Mechthild Hesse

Teenage Fiction in the Active English Classroom

Klett Lerntraining

For Emilia

Bildnachweis:
S. 70: Sharon Creech, "Love That Dog", Bloomsbury Publishing Plc,
S. 88, 107: Mechthild Hesse, S. 98, 111, 113: Mirko Bischler

Bibliografische Information der Deutschen Nationalbibliothek
Die Deutsche Nationalbibliothek verzeichnet diese Publikation in der Deutschen Nationalbibliografie; detaillierte bibliografische Daten sind im Internet über http://dnb.d-nb.de abrufbar.

Auflage 4. 3. 2. 1. | 2012 2011 2010 2009
Die letzten Zahlen bezeichnen jeweils die Auflage und das Jahr des Druckes.
Dieses Werk folgt der reformierten Rechtschreibung und Zeichensetzung. Ausnahmen bilden Texte, bei denen künstlerische, philologische oder lizenzrechtliche oder andere Gründe einer Änderung entgegenstehen.
Das Werk und seine Teile sind urheberrechtlich geschützt. Jede Nutzung in anderen als den gesetzlich zugelassenen Fällen bedarf der vorherigen schriftlichen Einwilligung des Verlages. Hinweis zu §52a UrhG: Weder das Werk noch seine Teile dürfen ohne eine solche Einwilligung eingescannt und in ein Netzwerk eingestellt werden. Dies gilt auch für Intranets von Schulen und sonstigen Bildungseinrichtungen.
Fotomechanische Wiedergabe nur mit Genehmigung des Verlages.

© Klett Lerntraining GmbH, Stuttgart 2009
Alle Rechte vorbehalten.
www.klett.de/uniwissen
Redaktion: Manfred Ott
Umschlaggestaltung: Sabine Kaufmann
Umschlagbild: Oliver Lucht (Pfeffer und Salz), Freiburg
Satz: Kassler Grafik-Design, Leipzig
Druck: Druckerei Wirtz, Speyer
Printed in Germany
ISBN 978-3-12-939534-9

Table of Contents

1 Introduction — 6

    1 Why extensive reading is necessary in the EFL classroom — 6
    2 How the book is organized — 7
    3 Aims of the book — 8
    4 Why so many American sources? — 9
    5 Using appropriate terms for "Jugendliteratur" — 10
    6 Using first person personal pronouns — 10
    7 Learners' exposure to teenage fiction at school — 11
    8 Selecting adequate books for entire classes — 12
    9 The problem of gender differences, gender similarities and individual differences — 13

2 Young adult fiction for EFL learners — 17

    1 Why fiction? — 17
    2 Picture books, comics and graphic novels — 21
    3 Problem novels — 34
    4 Multicultural novels — 38
    5 Historical fiction — 41
    6 Adventure, animal and survival fiction — 47
    7 Mystery: crime and detective novels — 49
    8 Fantasy — 52
    9 Ghost and horror stories — 60
    10 Superheroes — 62
    11 Short stories — 67
    12 Verse novels — 69
    13 A note on poetry, drama and non-fiction — 72

3 Young adult fiction for foreign language development — 78

    1 Intercultural communicative competence — 78
    2 Tasks and teachers — 81
        1 Tasks — 81
        2 Teachers — 85
    3 Improving "receptive" and "productive" skills — 87
        1 Reading — 87
        2 Listening — 90
        3 Speaking — 91
        4 Writing — 96

4 Suggestions for literary projects — 104

    1 Identification, empathy and change of perspective in acting — 104
    2 Learning through watching, listening and responding — 111

5 Reading with weak, reluctant readers — 114

    1 What weak, mostly male, reluctant readers want — 114
    2 Reading material for weak, reluctant readers — 116
    3 Individual reading: Working with book boxes — 117
    4 Funding book boxes — 118

6 Class libraries and beyond — 120

    1 The book box at the Realschule Kirchzarten — 120
    2 Activities for the entire school to promote reading — 126
    3 Summary and outlook — 128

Bibliography — 131

Index — 146

Preface

„Reading Is It!"

Among the many films with educational content, none has stood out as much as *Rhythm Is It!*, which appeared on German and international screens in 2004. It shows 250 Berlin high school students – many of them academically weaker students from 25 different nations – dancing Strawinsky's "Sacre du Printemps" on stage. In 2002, two English artists, Sir Simon Rattle, the conductor of the Berliner Philharmonie and the choreographer Royston Maldoom had started the experiment to give students a new sense of self by leading them beyond their limited personal experiences. Above all, the documentary mirrors the process of how these otherwise reluctant and unmotivated high school students went from being self-conscious youths who did not expect much of themselves to being proud, self-confident human beings.

Rhythm Is It!, a model for the reading classroom

There are basically two factors that triggered this process: Two highly artistically gifted, socially committed "teachers" (choreographer and conductor) and two media that finally managed to fascinate students (music and dance). But neither classical music nor ballet dance were part of the students' lives. Royston Maldoom, the choreographer, himself a "difficult" school kid, worked hardest with the youngsters. Having done similar projects with disadvantaged youths, with street kids in Ethiopia, and juvenile delinquents in England, he believed in the Berlin students' potential; he had a hard grip on them; he challenged them.

I am convinced that this can be a model for teachers promoting reading as well, although reading is an activity in which readers first have to sit still. Nonetheless, the way the material is dealt with can be action dominated and may very well require movement (see chapters 7 and 9). The material can be fascinating (see chapter 5). The books' contents do not have to remain in the realm of what children already know. It can and should go beyond it; it should show children other worlds outside their very limited personal and social reality. (Almost all highly popular youth literature at the turn of the millennium is fantasy literature, way beyond and above readers' lives.) And with fascinating literature and "action strategies", teachers should challenge their students.

Special thanks to Helen Joujan and Susanne Heinz for her helpful proofreading of the manuscript, Ansgar Nünning for his good advice, Manfred Ott for his careful editing, Carlin Senf for checking the literature list and the index.

Mechthild Hesse
September 2009

Introduction

1 Why extensive reading is necessary in the EFL classroom

Changing learners – changing teaching

Today's English learners are different from the learners of only 10 years ago. Every student knows nowadays that to be "up-to-date", to get around in the world, or even to be hired by an international company, he/she has to have a certain level of English competency. English has become the global language, the language of information and communication.

Learners are used to the ubiquity of English, especially since they have discovered the internet. The internet is an excellent source of information, but learners have to learn how to retrieve this information, as it often is presented, sometimes hidden, in relatively long texts. A battle is raging about the way reading should be viewed: whether reading is reading of only printed or of electronic texts as well, whether teenagers read more or less while being increasingly involved with the internet, and whether the way they read is beneficial or detrimental to their overall literacy (cf. MARLER 2008). I assert that exposure to all kinds of reading is necessary to make people literate.

The "PISA" study has shown that one major function of reading is to prepare students for the task of retrieving information and responding to it critically. The OECD study has neglected literature to a certain extent, but it has nevertheless shown that reading motivation and reading strategies are necessary to reach this goal (cf. DEUTSCHES PISA-KONSORTIUM 2001). And this has to be trained until the strategies can finally be applied automatically. What is more inviting than practicing and using them in connection with motivating stories?

Acquiring reading literacy through stories

Why stories? Stories are a part of human life. Stories appeal to all ages. Stories may tell us much about ourselves as well as about our own and foreign cultures. The cultural information of a narrative embeds itself in our memory much better because stories are holistic; they appeal not only to our intellect but also to our senses and our hearts. And stories are challenging! Although fiction takes up most of chapter 5 on literary genres, I have added a section on non-fiction, knowing that there is a large number of readers, especially males, who prefer information books. And is history not called "story" sometimes as well?

The "stories" can also be visual "texts" such as comics, picture stories, films and video clips, games or oral sources like audio books, radio plays, and songs. But due to the limitations of this book, I will mainly focus on print material. Where appropriate, I will point to other media, mainly film, related to the printed texts.

2 How the book is organized

The book is divided into two main parts: the literature part, in which readers will be introduced to young adult (YA) literature genres and their appropriateness for the EFL classroom (chapter 2) and the teaching literature part, dealing with concrete tasks and projects for implementing teen literature in the intermediate secondary classroom at the *Sekundarstufe* I level (chapter 3–6).

Getting to know current YA fiction – teaching current YA fiction

In the first section, YA genres for grades 5–10 will be presented and books from that genre will be evaluated. For every genre there will be concrete book recommendations for advanced learners of the *Sekundarstufe* I (grades 9–10), intermediate learners (grade 7–8), and for younger learners (grades 5–6), as well as for reluctant readers. Some notes on novels for males and females have also been added (see also chapter 4). Some of the books for grades 9 and 10 can easily be read in grade 11 as well. This categorization is only a very broad guideline for practicing and future teachers; everybody knows that each class is different.

Fiction and its sub-genres

The second section (chapters 3–6) will focus on the questions of teaching YA literature. What could the everyday "reading classroom" look like? Which skills are being trained and promoted with which approaches and methods? What kinds of projects are suitable for reaching goals that the methodology of teaching literature is aiming at?

The YA fiction classroom – skills and projects

I am especially concerned about "reluctant readers". These are either weak readers or learners who do not like reading, read very little or not at all in their spare time, but would be good if they were exposed to motivating texts. Chapter 5 is dedicated to this specific group.

Reluctant readers

I consider this book with its recommendations a first step towards a kind of "story curriculum" that might help teachers to build on appropriate stories that learners may be exposed to in their first six years of secondary schools. I recommend stories and novels that should attract the attention of many learners, because they are suspenseful, informative, funny, and creative. These are stories which offer ways for young learners and teenagers of both genders to learn the English language by reading both in class and individually. These stories allow them to learn more about other cultures (and thus learn more about their own culture) and about other children's and young adults' experiences. All of these learning opportunities should help them to become mature human beings (BUSHMAN & PARKS 2003).

Story curriculum for the Secondary I level

Some of the stories seem to be challenging for young learners, yet haven't we learned through the "Harry Potter experience" that young people

The challenge of books!

Chapter 1 Introduction

like a challenge, if it is the right one? Who would have thought 10 years ago that youngsters would wait eagerly for the next *Harry Potter* or *Twilight* novel to come out and devour 1000 pages in the foreign language? (cf. GASCHKE 2007)

The appeal of verse novels

Some of the books presented here are "verse novels", novels written in poetic form. I know that many teachers have been turned off of poetry, mostly because of an exaggerated focus on poetry analysis. However, all of these poetic novels tell stories from a variety of perspectives. The form provides very profound insights into the characters themselves with relatively few words. The novels can be read quickly, often in one sitting. This way adolescents and teachers who think they do not like poetry can read interesting stories in a very short time. In my experience, students are often surprised at how easy this kind of free verse is and how touching the lives of the protagonists are (cf. HESSE 07).

3 Aims of the book

Target groups

The book is targeted at university students and professors, student teachers and teacher trainers, and teachers at various levels: at university, in the second phase of student teaching (*Referendariat*) and practicing teachers at the high school level, in all kinds of German high schools from *Hauptschule* to *Gymnasium*. It has completely different goals than KULLMANN's *Englische Kinder- und Jugendliteratur* (2008) or PETER HUNT's *Children's Literature. An Illustrated History* (1995). Both give a good overview of mostly classical and very well-known English children's literature, whereas I focus predominantly on current YA literature.

This book serves as an overview of current texts, materials, tasks, and an array of projects that may accompany the reading classroom. It may also be used in English as a Second Language (ESL) contexts abroad since most books are authentic (there are only very few recommendations for simplified texts) and many of the materials and ideas stem from international sources (mostly American, British, and Canadian).

Goals

This book has several goals:
- ▶ to encourage teachers to use more motivating, longer literary texts instead of being too fixated on "textbooks" or "course books" (*Lehrwerke*)
- ▶ to reduce students' and teachers' fears of longer texts in the EFL classrooms
- ▶ to encourage teachers to challenge their students with motivating texts
- ▶ to make readers aware of the large variety of interesting children's and YA literature that can be used in the EFL secondary classroom and give recommendations
- ▶ to make teachers avid readers

- to show that reading literature expands students' knowledge of the world, giving them a new awareness of their own world and thus offering a great potential for intercultural learning
- to help improve students' reading skills so that they are better prepared for such real-life tasks as retrieving information and joining international discussion groups
- to show that with appropriate additional materials and motivating student-centered tasks and projects, reading YA literature may be pleasurable for both learners and teachers
- to demonstrate and prove that even slower learners (many at German *Real-* and *Hauptschule* levels) gain knowledge and skills when dealing with motivating texts
- to encourage teachers to make "silent reading" possible and to have classroom libraries with a variety of easy and popular books and magazines.

4 Why so many American sources?

There are three main reasons why such a variety of US American sources is used: Americans, especially well-known American JACK ZIPES, Fulbright professor and author of many books on children's and teenage literature, and various American authors and librarians have taught me about the richness of American children's and YA literature.

The richness of American children's literature

American YA literature markets a large variety of books so that readers get a good understanding of the seemingly so similar but actually very different American culture, which has undoubtedly had a very strong impact on youths all over the world, and definitely on German youths.

The "otherness" of American children's literature

North Americans realized much earlier than Germans that a specific group of "non-readers", the "reluctant readers", has to be addressed: With the comprehensive high school system in North America and in teachers' action research, the reluctant reader – often male – has been taken into account much earlier than in Germany (cf. BROZO 2002; MILLARD 1997; SMITH & WILHELM 2002; WILHELM 1997).

American research of "reluctant" readers

Whereas many American teacher researchers like BROZO, SMITH & WILHELM focus on boys' reading, German PFEIFER ET AL. have provided us with information on girls' reading in the German *Hauptschule*. These studies were done with native speakers, but the American reading researcher KRASHEN (1997) also gives us interesting insight into English as a foreign language (EFL) reading classrooms.

Hauptschüler can be(come) readers too!

The American perspective is transcended many times as well, when I refer to other English speaking sources, mainly British and Canadian writers. Australian and New Zealand writers and their stories are only occasionally mentioned, but if then they are referred to with highest praise (e.g. *The Book Thief*).

5 Using appropriate terms for "Jugendliteratur"

Children's literature, teenage-, juvenile-, young adult fiction – which is the right term?

How easy it is to use the German term *Kinder- und Jugendliteratur* and how difficult to translate it! I will use the term *children's literature* when I refer to literature for children up to about twelve years of age. The terms *teenage fiction, juvenile fiction, young adult fiction* and *youth fiction* are used as synonyms. They refer to books for teenagers up to the age of nineteen! This is only a very broad and not always maintainable categorization. Many of the books formerly targeted at young adults are now read by children, and some of the books for children and young adults are read by adults, too. When speaking about authors of this genre, I mostly call them *children's authors* for practical reasons.

6 Using first person personal pronouns

Action research

Much of the following text is based on research combined with experience. As I was a long-time high school teacher who taught all kinds of learners on the secondary I and secondary II levels, all of the research that I did was action research, a research concept based on reflecting one's own teaching experience in order to improve one's own actions (cf. ALTRICHTER & POSCH 1994). At the university level, we continue doing action research projects with students (cf. chapter 6.1).

"I" and "we" as indicators of "my" experience-based action research

Therefore I frequently use the first person personal pronouns "I" and "we" to show that what I am writing is based on my own personal experience. In this respect, too, I am following North American writers who do not only refer to their own personal experiences, but also emphasize their personal tastes, opinions, and the process in which these might change.

The example of North American experts

Like the Canadians NODELMAN & REIMER (2003: 3f.), two well-known children's literature experts, I want to emphasize that not only the experiences that I am describing, but even my novel evaluations are based on personal taste and opinion that may differ from those of my readers. However, I do dare to give advice to young people or people who are less experienced in using YA literature in the classroom. I also make my criteria for the book selection clear so that readers know the preconditions.

7 Learners' exposure to teenage fiction at school

In ALAN BENNETT's highly hilarious *The Uncommon Reader* (2008: 29), The English Queen, the "uncommon reader" herself, says after having accidentally discovered the joy of reading: "Books are not about passing the time. They're about other lives. Other worlds. Far from wanting time to pass one just wishes one had more of it." *The Uncommon Reader* is all about the enjoyment of reading, which causes a sudden change in The Queen's life, who becomes an advocate of reading books rather late in life. She is fascinated by the "indifference" of literature: "Books did not care who was reading them or whether one read them or not. All readers were equal, herself included. Literature, she thought, is a common wealth; letters a republic. It was anonymous; it was shared; it was common" (30f.).
As much as The Queen becomes "contagious" with her enthusiasm, teachers' love of literature may infect their learners. Teachers are and always have been role models for their pupils.

Books as an "indifferent" medium for exploring the world

In our culture, where reading competes with a great number of other – and supposedly more attractive – pastime activities, young people should at least be exposed to, confronted with and experience the large variety of fascinating YA literature (variety of genres, language and vernacular, styles, and themes) at school. If they begin with teenage fiction at the secondary I level (*Mittelstufe*), students will be much better prepared for the more challenging adult texts at the secondary II level (*Oberstufe*). Thus fewer students will have to refer to *Lernhilfen* or English "Cliff Notes" or similar notes, whose impressive sales figures are usually based on students' fear of these difficult adult texts.

Young adult literature as preparation for adult literature

Teachers' enthusiasm alone, however, does not turn non-readers into readers. So much depends on the approaches and methods used in the EFL classroom, which should be a fear-free zone, a space without an "affective filter" (KRASHEN 1997), in which a variety of methods will be applied that meet young people's interests (including their inclination to electronic media). The young learner's fear of long texts with a relatively large amount of unknown vocabulary must be met with a positive, encouraging, student-centered, student-activating approach. Such an approach makes learners quickly realize how much more they actually do understand than they initially thought. And how proud young learners are after having finished and understood their first English book, written for native speakers and not for non-native learners!

The reading classroom as a "fear-free zone"

From my point of view, that of a teacher who regularly taught young adult literature from grade 9 on, learners are supposed to:
▶ enjoy literature dealing with the lives of young people in target countries

What YA fiction can offer learners

Chapter 1   Introduction

- read about adolescents from other cultures having similar or different encounters with others, dealing with similar or different problems
- develop some kind of relationship to, understanding of, empathy for or even identification with the protagonists
- test their knowledge of English with long, authentic texts written for native speakers
- expand their English language competences
- be motivated to read, hear and listen to more
- …

> **TIP**
> *Reflect again on the reasons why children's and YA literature should be read in the EFL classroom. Put the arguments into a ranking system according to your own view.*
> *Bring forth arguments for teachers who strictly follow textbooks and parents who judge their children's success by how many textbook units they have covered.*
> *Read other books such as "Black Boy" by Richard Wright who speaks about the power of reading for a disadvantaged black kid like himself.*

8 Selecting adequate books for entire classes

The problem of book selection

Selecting appropriate books is not an easy task, especially since the book market for young people is ever expanding. One reason why I wrote this book is to represent a large variety of novels for all ages and levels in secondary schools. This was only possible through the help of native speaking authors, teachers, and librarians. Most children's authors in the USA speak to classes in schools, in libraries and even in shopping malls. When English writer DAVID ALMOND (*Skellig*) spoke to young middle school students (grades 5–7) in a Seattle shopping mall in 2004, he asked the young audience who wanted to become a writer and a lot of hands went up. These children from an ordinary public school had obviously read some of ALMOND's work, were interested in both the stories and in the author, and asked him many questions. The wish to become writers themselves came only after they had been exposed to a number of books.

Selection criteria

But which books are appropriate for EFL learners? What kinds of books should a teacher select who wants to read with a whole class? Which guidelines should be used when selecting books? The following list of selection criteria should help teachers before the selection:

- Is the large majority of students in the class able to understand the text without stumbling over a large number of unknown words? Of course, it is best for teachers to either use annotated texts or provide lists of key words that need to be understood. The percentage of unknown words should not exceed 1.8 – 3.6% (cf. KAST 1985: 158f.).

- Is the story believable or imaginable? (Is it coherent, logical?)
- Will a large number of students be able to relate to, empathize or even identify with the characters? Even feeling superior to characters and looking down on them is a relationship (cf. TABBERT 1997a: 5).
- Is the text interesting, exciting or even thrilling? Maybe it is funny, too?
- How well can students visualize what is happening? Is there additional material (music, pictures, film etc.) that may support comprehension?
- Do students learn something about the target culture and can they use their knowledge of their own culture as a basis for intercultural learning?
- If texts are not about the other culture, are there human relationships or other issues they can relate to?
- Can students compare and contrast their own lives with the lives of the young protagonists they encounter in the texts?
- Can a large variety of student-centered tasks be created so that learners are able to use their own knowledge and creativity?

> **TIP** *Research other selection criteria lists, i.e. the one in NÜNNING & SURKAMP 2006: 49f. Compare and discuss them with your study group and make a list of your own.*

9 The problem of gender differences, gender similarities and individual differences

Book selection definitely becomes even more difficult when gender differences are taken into account. Many males have clearly distinct tastes, inclinations, and interests, whereas particular reading preferences for girls are not as obvious. There is a general understanding that girls will read boys' books, but boys will not read girls' books. Why this may be the case is explained by physician and psychologist LEONARD SAX's research showing that boys in general have much stronger preferences from an early age on, as young as 9 months old (cf. 2006: 27). According to SAX, gender differences are based on differences in brain activity. Therefore, he postulates that the "gender blindness" prevailing in educational institutions since the 1970s has to end.

Gender differences

Especially since boys read less, are weaker readers (DEUTSCHES PISA KONSORTIUM 2001: 256) and the amount of reading even drops in late adolescence, special attention has to be directed at boys' reading. Reading research has found that boys prefer information books, fast-paced adventure, science fiction, horror, mystery, all of which may also include both violence and humor. What most of them do not like are the problem novel and the relationship novel (cf. NEWKIRK 2002: 70, 110; MILLARD 1997: 61; MILLARD 2001; SAX 2006: 59; 106ff.).

Boys' reading preferences

Chapter 1   Introduction

Boys' books' heroes

Boys want books with "strong male characters who take dramatic action to change their world" (SAX 112). These books should be fun and should have a closer connection to real life. Therefore SMITH & WILHELM have titled their classroom research book dealing with male reading: "*Reading Don't Fix No Chevys*" (2002).

NEWKIRK (2002: 70ff.) argues that in addition to information books, newspapers, and magazines, boys have a "romance" with "pure" facts represented in sports tables and lists of team standings. His observations are supported by statistics of the OECD "PISA" study, according to which boys perform equally well at reading tables, graphs, maps and schematic drawings, whereas reading and interpreting continuous texts is clearly a girls' domain (255).

Whereas SAX promotes the reading of classics with strong male characters like *Huckleberry Finn* for boys, NEWKIRK criticizes advocates of classical literature. Although NEWKIRK praises classical literature for its "popular elements", such as crude jokes, allusions to sex etc., he strongly disagrees with the advocates of the classics who look down on information books, funny books and comics calling these genres "subliterature" (70). As a teacher-researcher, he wants to include entertaining literature such as satire and parody, generally loved by boys, into the reading classroom.

Classroom tasks for boys

Therefore the reading classroom activities should not be too problem- and reflection-oriented and should not require extensive analysis of character development, which, according to SAX, teachers' materials are full of. After SAX this is one important reason why boys usually dislike the reading done at school. SAX (108) extends his criticism of "feeling-oriented" tasks to role plays as well, which stands in contrast to practising teachers' classroom research (SMITH & WILHELM's 2002).

Girls' reading preferences

To my knowledge not much reading research is currently being done on girls' reading, most likely because girls are not considered at-risk readers. However, PIEPER ET AL.'s (2004) research with female "non-readers" (Frankfurt *Hauptschülerinnen*) shows that although they generally acknowledge the value of reading, reading never was and is part of their lives. In that respect, they are no different from weak male readers. The authors suspect that reading done at school did nothing to close the "inequality gap" existing in the selective German school system, which was also criticized by the "PISA" study (355ff.).

What if girls' preferences had been taken into account? Girls do prefer fiction to non-fiction, relationship and problem novels to science fiction, horror novels, newspapers and magazines. Girls want to get caught up in a story; they want to identify with protagonists; and if they do, they do not even mind reading longer books (see girls' fascination with MEYER's voluminous *Twilight* trilogy). Especially teen romance is popular among girls. KRASHEN refers to research showing that these kinds of

9 The problem of gender differences, gender similarities and individual differences

books led the girls to read other genres later and made them library users (cf. 2004: 111ff.).

In the recommendations (chapter 2) I have tried to take gender differences into account (see the category "boys' books, girls' books") in order to help teachers find books for either single-sex classes or for silent, individual reading inside and outside class. Chapter 5 will present reading materials, teaching methods, and suggestions to specifically motivate weak, reluctant readers.

Novels for both genders for silent reading

Since the main focus of this book is on literature for both genders and since we are first of all concerned with a coeducational reading classroom that involves all learners, books presented here are to appeal to both sexes. Looking at popular novels for both genders one can probably deduce that both boys and girls prefer rather fast-paced books that involve some action with protagonists and plots they can relate to. Ideal books for coeducational classes are probably the ones involving a female and a male protagonist.
Having mixed audiences in mind today's children's authors often write their stories from two narrators' perspectives, one being a girl, the other a boy (*Abomination, Dear Nobody, Armageddon Summer*) or even use multiple narrators' perspectives (*Give a Boy a Gun, Keesha's House, Bull Run, The Simple Gift*). Such novels seem most appropriate for the coeducational classroom.

Novels for entire classes

To make novels interesting for both boys and girls, authors often choose a male character as a protagonist, who possesses universal human traits, is exposed to universal problems, and who courageously fights for his own and other people's freedom (see *The Giver* chapter 5.8).

Male characters dealing with universal problems

But contemporary authors also want to tell about girls' courage in adventure stories. Adventure and survival novels such as Frost's *Diamond Willow*, a story of a girl who saves her dog in a secret flight through the Alaskan wilderness, will probably be read with suspense by both boys and girls. In fiction, too, some girls – like boys – take risks, are prone to overestimating their abilities, and consequently put themselves and others in danger (Sax 45). In Margaret Haddix's *Among the Hidden*, it is the girl protagonist who leads other forbidden third children into a dangerous demonstration, in which many of them lose their lives, whereas the boy protagonist is wise and stays hidden.
Like the authors mentioned above, many current children's writers writing more demanding fiction try to avoid gender stereotypes. Not flat, stereotypical boys and girls, but round characters, protagonists with contradictory feelings and conflicting individual character traits are portrayed.

Female characters having universal character traits

Chapter 1   Introduction

This is the literature that is best suited for mixed classes. If teachers are not sure about the class' likes and dislikes they should have students select their own books from a number of novels the teacher suggests. Excerpts from various novels (cf. Hesse 2003) can be read in groups using the "expert puzzle" method (cf. chapter 1.8) so that every member of the class will be able to contribute to a democratic class decision.

> **TIP**
> *Design questionnaires and/or carry out interviews with male and female students you teach/have taught to ask what kinds of books they read. Compare the answers with what is said above about boys' reading and girls' reading. Make two different lists, one for boys and one for girls.*
> *Find out in how far boys and girls have similar interests.*

Young adult fiction for EFL learners   2

1 Why fiction?

Fiction is defined as an "imaginary narrative created by an author, not a record of fact. All fiction is imaginative, but the genre determines how true to real life the work must be to be plausible." (LATROBE ET AL. 2002: 71f. as cited in KASTEN 2005: 178). Here we are reminded of two elements: although imaginary fiction is contrasted to factual non-fiction, it has to be plausible to be accepted by readers.

Definition

Fiction comprises the largest segment of the YA literature field. There are poetry and drama as well, but these genres are not as popular and – as separate YA genres – will only be touched upon in this context (see chapter 2,13). GOODNOW (2007) speaks of the new popularity of YA fiction which the market has not experienced since the 1940s. In spite of teenagers' occupation with electronic media, books seem to have a special appeal, at least to a large number of young people who have the means to buy books. Most people complain about teenagers' decreasing reading time, but one has to remember that a large number of young people in their teens today were brought up with books to a much greater extent than youths were in earlier decades.

New popularity of YA fiction

The recent popularity of YA fiction is probably due to several factors: Firstly, it is the universal appeal of stories; whether they are true or just imagined does not really play a role. MADELEINE L'ENGLE, author of the classic *A Wrinkle in Time*, the 1962 Newbery Award winner, calls fiction "a vehicle for truth", saying that truth and story is what connect human beings to each other (KASTEN ET AL. 176). Stories are part of our lives and of human existence. Creation stories, stories of religious and mythical figures, etc. make up people's beliefs. Myths represent civilizations, nations, and tribes. Fairy tales originate from national or regional folklore. Historical fiction deals with people in certain historical periods. Some stories are serious, some are funny, and often the tone is mixed. The earliest stories were narrated orally, later told and retold on paper and changed according to the narrators', the listeners', and the society's needs. This should remind us of the universal importance of stories for humankind anywhere.

The appeal of stories for humans

Secondly, this appeal seems to have something to do with "make-believe", something we humans sometimes need in order to distance ourselves from our real lives, lose ourselves in stories and get help from them. In *Brooklyn Follies*, PAUL AUSTER retells an episode involving an interaction between Kafka and a small girl who is devastated because she has lost her doll. He consoles her by telling her that the doll has written a letter to him to say she has gone on a trip. He promises to bring the letter to the park the following day. For the next three weeks after

Make-believe of stories

that incident Kafka meets the little girl in the park every day and reads her another of the doll's letters, which he carefully prepares at home. The doll goes to school, grows up, meets other people, has some complications in her life, later marries, and says good-bye to a lifelong friend. Gradually Kafka prepares the little girl for the time when the doll vanishes from her life forever. By that time, the girl does not miss the doll any more. With a story Kafka has cured her of her unhappiness. "She has the story, and when a person is lucky enough to live inside a story, to live in an imaginary world the pains of this world disappear. For as long as the story goes on, reality no longer exists." (AUSTER 156).

Easy availability of books

Thirdly, the appeal of young adult literature has something to do with a bulging population of teens who were brought up on books and the market now provides them with a large variety of literature, from "chick lit" and formulaic series to more challenging, creative literature that tries to avoid clichés.

Young adults as implied readers

A growing YA market targeting teens and young adults

In an rapidly growing YA market, which has developed at an ever increasing pace since the 1960s, many writers have a clear idea of which audience they are writing for. For most YA writers, teenagers are the "implied readers" (ISER 1972). However, sometimes they may have dual audiences in mind or the novels end up being read by several audiences, and therefore publishers market them in separate sections, maybe even with different dust jackets. This was the case with several novels appearing in recent years, for example ZUSAK's *The Book Thief* (2007) and BOYNE's *The Boy in the Striped Pyjamas* (2006), two very unusual and extraordinary novels about the Holocaust. Meanwhile, *The Boy in the Striped Pyjamas* has appeared on the screen (2008) and the film *The Book Thief* is in the making. After the first success of LOIS LOWRY's *The Giver* as a children's book in the USA, it was published as an adult edition as well.

Young – adult-crossover novels

The YA market is providing an ever increasing number of long, challenging books. After the appearance of ROWLING's *Harry Potter* series, a variety of other long, challenging books were published. ZUSAK's *The Book Thief*, ANDERSON's two novels *Octavian Nothing* and *Feed*, PULLMAN's *His Dark Materials*, CHAMBERS' *This Is All* – to name only a few examples – constitute a "crossover genre", a genre that is dissolving the frontier between adult and juvenile fiction (cf. J. HUNT 2007, HITCHENS 2002). These books are characterized by a more demanding and sophisticated use of language, increasingly experimental narrative forms, as well as demanding, ironic, ambivalent young adult and adult characters. In addition, more mature themes, worlds where good and evil coexist, where frequent allusions are made to other works, ideas, or times, and above all, where authors "make no concessions and no compromises, do not condescend to their readers, speak to them as people rather than as teenagers". The crossover novel requires of young readers more concentration and "helps move them from the pleasures of light reading to the pleasures of literary reading" (J. HUNT without p.; cf. GASCHKE). Books for children, PULLMAN asserts, should be "about how to grow up," not about how to remain childish (cf. HITCHENS).

Books for dual readerships may eventually become classics since they can be read and understood differently at various stages in life. This is even the case with picture books. For example, children will probably not understand the allusions to Magritte in ANTHONY BROWNE's picture book *My Dad*, yet they enjoy the story itself. In PULLMAN's *His Dark Materials*, adults with the knowledge of Milton and Blake will probably enjoy the references to them and what they might mean (cf. NODELMAN & REIMER 21).

Dual readerships

Teaching with stories
If stories have such an appeal to today's youngsters, why do we not use more stories and novels in the EFL classroom?
One rather simple answer is: because teaching goes through historical phases. The Reader Response Theory, based on the works of LOUISE ROSENBLATT (1938) and WOLFGANG ISER (1972), was not discovered for the purposes of reading and teaching literature until the 1980s (BREDELLA 1989; HUNFELD 1982; NISSEN 1985). And when it was transformed and adapted to reading at school, it first addressed the needs of advanced learners (BREDELLA & LEGUTKE 1986; BREDELLA 1996). Except for NISSEN's 1988 article on young adult novels and his list of recommendations, the youth novel's potential for teaching younger learners was "discovered" mainly in the last two decades, during which time the Reader Response Theory played a major role, and was even applied to teaching younger learners. It takes readers more seriously than ever before.

Teaching literature – a relatively recent part of the EFL classroom

Reader response principles (simplified):
▶ Texts do not exist without readers.
▶ The reader makes meaning from what he/she reads.
▶ The reader reads for pleasure (cf. ROSENBLATT's "efferent reading") and for understanding (him- and herself and the world), and not for analysis.
▶ Reader and text interact. This means that the text (with its writer, his/her context, and the circumstances in which it is set) and the reader's knowledge of the world contribute to the reader's understanding of the text.
▶ The reader needs both involvement (identification, empathy, adoption of other perspectives) and a critical distance (cf. BREDELLA 1989). In adopting other perspectives, readers may see their own limitations (BREDELLA & BURWITZ-MELZER 2004).
▶ Through literature, readers learn more about others and themselves.

Taking the reader seriously

Chapter 2 Young adult fiction for EFL learners

Literature's developmental help

The reader response theory, which initially did not include foreign language learners, takes a holistic approach. It takes the idea seriously that adolescents need literature to help them become more mature human beings (BUSHMAN & PARKS 2003; NISSEN 1988).
Intercultural communicative competence, the highest aim of all English teaching (MÜLLER-HARTMANN & SCHOCKER-VON DITFURTH 2004; see chapter 3,1) is easier to achieve with authentic literature that is set in the target culture. Narrators tell their stories from their own perspectives and readers try to understand their points of view, the way they see life. This understanding is specifically necessary with first person narrators. This, however, does not mean that the novels have to be set in the foreign culture. Literature that could be set anywhere can also be a basis for intercultural learning (cf. chapter 3).

Teachers' strong textbook dependence

Another reason why not more literature is used in the secondary EFL classroom is the dependence of English teachers on textbooks (cf. NÜNNING & SURKAMP 2006: 44). And textbooks are based on the idea of English learning that can be planned and has a predictable progression. In many teachers' minds, textbooks have substituted the curriculum. The school curriculum is often just a breakdown of the textbook for a certain grade.

45-minute lesson dependence

Another reason can be found in German teacher training. Even now teachers' performance in teacher education is graded on the basis of a 45-minute lesson. Teacher training does not focus enough on teaching units.
In addition, the idea that teachers are not only instructors but also assistants helping young people develop well is not common ground on which English teachers operate. Their idea often is to teach just English vocabulary and grammar.

EFL teachers more than instructors

Rudolf Steiner schools (Waldorf schools) and other independent schools can help us see beyond the "vocabulary-grammar enclosure". Waldorf teachers who use no textbooks at all know that stories are necessary for the development of (young) people. They know about the universality of stories, focusing also on traditional stories, myths, and classics in other subjects.

Focus on current Young Adult fiction

Yet I will not concentrate on traditional stories, although I know how important they are. I will refer to classical tales only when dealing with comic books and graphic novels (see chapter 2). My main focus is on stories written in the last 30 years. The books that I present here are books that today's teenagers should easily relate to. Except for some simplified readers, most of the books were written for natives. But my intention is to promote them for young EFL or ESL learners who want to learn the English used by their modern day native speaking peers (cf. HESSE 2002). I will focus on easily accessible literature, including some genres such as comics or romance novels that are sometimes looked down upon condescendingly (see chapter 5). The main idea is to provide motivating literature for today's young learners of English.

> **TIP**
> Stories do not have to be read quietly; they can also be told orally. Practice storytelling with and without the help of pictures. In class you will see that listeners become quiet and love the quiet listening phases. Make storytelling a ritual in class. In doing so you will lay the foundation for your students interest in more and more stories.

2 Picture books, comics and graphic novels

Like stories, pictures are commonly seen as expressions of the human experience and are thus as universal as stories. The earliest humans left traces of picture stories on walls of caves as accounts of their culture. In his guide to graphic novels, PAWUK (without page) explains the importance of pictures for human beings in a comic book style: The comic artist makes fun of the absurd gap between the wide ranging acceptance and importance of picture books for children and the condemnation of picture books for young adults and even adults. Inferring from the popularity of television, we can say that our culture is visual and that pictures seem to be appealing to both children and adults. In the following, I will go into more detail on the art and design of picture books.

Pictures as expressions of human experiences

Picture books
Picture books, unlike illustrated books, cannot be understood without the pictures, for words and images interact. One cannot exist without the other; verbal and visual communication "constitute an indivisible whole" (NIKOLAJEVA in: ZIPES 3: 248).

The art of picture books

KASTEN ET AL. call picture books "the marriage of literature and fine arts into a unique literary form" (147), referring to MAURICE SENDAK, the great creator of *Where the Wild Things Are* (*Wo die wilden Kerle wohnen*), whose pictures "vivify, quicken, and vitalize" (1988: 3). But it is not only this. *Where the Wild Things Are* (1963) changed the concept of picture books thematically, aesthetically, and psychologically. Not only do the images support the few sentences, but they reflect the inner world of a young child who cannot express his feelings with words. SENDAK mirrors the emotional state of the character by using three wordless double spreads to illustrate "the wild rumpus" (cf. ibid.: 248).
The book is an example of a picture book that was wholly done by one artist. SENDAK wrote the story and drew the pictures, whereas today the

The art of MAURICE SENDAK

vast majority of picture books are done by collaborations of two people, a writer and an illustrator. However, the best examples of picture book creations are the ones done by a single picture book maker, such as BRIGG, BROWNE, BURNINGHAM, CARLE, and STEIG (cf. ibid.: 249).

Just as there are easier and more difficult novels, there are also less complex and more complex picture books. NODELMAN & REIMER (2003: 274) point out that even picture stories for children are not necessarily easier to understand than stories without pictures, since picture comprehension depends much on cultural conventions and cultural knowledge. For example, a Western reader can only fully comprehend the much acclaimed Newbery Medal winning graphic novel *American-born Chinese*, if he/she has an understanding of Chinese mythology.

Visual literacy

But not only is cultural knowledge needed for picture book comprehension, a kind of visual literacy is necessary as well. Only because children are exposed to a lot of images in today's visual culture, are they often very sophisticated interpreters of pictures (ibid. 276). Readers of picture books are meant to focus on how the pictures relate to the accompanying words and to the pictures preceding and following them. Readers and viewers must consider not only the beauty of the pictures, but also how the pictures contribute to an unfolding knowledge of which they are a part (cf. ibid.: 278). With pictures drawing attention to the moment and text hinting at what is to come, the reader's reading pace is slowed down and his/her response is triggered (cf. TABBERT 1997b: 19).

Art and design of illustrations

Elements of picture book design

Teachers who use picture books in the classroom should not only have a basic understanding of the relationship between words and pictures, but should also know a little bit about the visual design. Every element of an illustrator's design is of importance, from front cover to blurb, from the dedication page to the final page. The artistic design consists of many elements that have to be considered:

Lines

Lines are used to show what is painted or drawn. Lines show movement, shape, and texture; they show feeling, mood, and atmosphere. Uncompleted lines are seen as unstable, completed ones as reassuring (cf. ibid.: 282)

Color

Color also reflects tone and mood, setting, or cultural aspects. Multicultural books, for example, are usually very colorful (cf. *The Hatseller and the Monkeys*, an African story). The use of primary colors and secondary colors, of bright, warm colors like red and yellow and cool colors like blue and green is never random. The use of black and white suggests seriousness, factual documentary truth, probably since it is used for newspapers.

Shapes – intersecting lines, for example – may depict size (small vs. large) as well as mood and tone. Shapes in ARMSTRONG's *Audubon* reflect vast pristine forests. Small people in front of huge objects may suggest loneliness, modesty, and snugness (cf. BROWNE's *My Dad*). Rounded shapes are associated with softness, whereas angular shapes stand for orderliness and rigidity.

Shapes

Borders of pages are more important than one might think. "Events seen through strictly defined boundaries imply detachment and objectivity" (ibid. 280). The white borders in VAN ALLSBURG's *The Polar Express* add some documentary-like truth to the otherwise fantastic events. Sometimes tension is created by breaking through borders like in RATHMAN's *Officer Buckle and Gloria*. Variation in borders shifts meaning. When Max gets into trouble in *Where the Wild Things Are*, SENDAK draws small pictures surrounded by white border space. As Max's independence grows, the pictures become larger and the borders smaller.

Borders

Symbols, codes, and gestures are sometimes only understood with the appropriate cultural knowledge. If you don't know what a crucifix stands for, you might not understand KEEPING's *Through the Window*. People from the Western world often depict sad events in black and gray shades and hues (e.g. ROSEN's *Sad*), whereas Indians use white for mourning. Body postures like an upturned head means happiness, while a slumped head stands for depression. Picture books rely heavily on these conventional assumptions (cf. ibid.: 288). Other pictorial dynamics are also relevant: shapes and sizes of objects and persons and their location in the picture, the point of view, and the focus.

Symbols, codes, and gestures

Action and plot represented in picture books
Since stories are about movement and changes and pictures are fixed in space and can only show one moment in time, illustrators have a variety of means to represent action: incomplete actions suggest that readers imagine their completion. Action lines in cartoons that are repeated several times have the same function. Distorted body parts may imply speed. In most picture books readers move from one picture to the next, which asks the reader to imagine what happened in between. Of course, the words of the stories often provide information about what has happened between the pictures. But there are also picture books without words, such as TAN's *The Arrival*, which tells an immigration story. DE PAOLA's *Pancakes for Breakfast* tells about making pancakes and WIESNER's illustrations in *Tuesday* depict frogs flying through the air.

Movement in pictures

Picture book styles
Style is the combined effect of all elements mentioned above and many more all together. It develops out of all kinds of choices the artists make. Artists have their own styles, but they usually follow a certain trend established in art history.

Variety of picture book styles

Chapter 2　　　Young adult fiction for EFL learners

Expressionism　　Expressionism is used to depict feelings. Objects do not have to be portrayed realistically. It uses stark colors and lines to get the meaning across.

Impressionism　　Impressionist art evokes comfort, it tends to be dreamy and romantic. It may also be used as an ironic counterpoint as in CHARLOTTE ZOLOTOW's and SENDAK's *Mr. Rabbit and the Lovely Present*, where the text with its jaunty, staccato style does not match the pictures (cf. ibid. 285).

Realism　　Realism mirrors reality as we see it in everyday life. Situations and characters seem authentic.

Surrealism　　Surrealist art evokes strangeness. Artists like Dali or Magritte "depict unrealistic situations in a highly representational way that makes the impossible seem strangely possible" (ibid. 284f.). Books often use a great deal of visual puns, which create an eerie atmosphere. In *Willy the Dreamer*, BROWNE, who makes frequent references to Magritte's art in his pictures, uses the style to confirm the nature of Willy's dreams. The monkey dreams that he could be everything: from a scuba diver to a king.

Naïve or folk art　　**Naïve or folk art** is often used by self-taught artists with no formal training. It uses a lot of tiny details and color.

National or cultural styles　　**National or cultural styles** are used by illustrators for tales from countries around the world (cf. DIAKITÉ's *The Hatseller and the Monkeys*).

Mixture of styles　　Some artists also allude to a variety of other styles. BROWNE's pictures not only include parts of Magritte's objects, such as the banana or a hat with the inscription "This is not a hat", but he also paints Willy in a jungle that is similar to Rousseau's jungles. TAN draws images of immigration that include realist photographic styles as well as a surrealistic, symbolic style.

Mostly it is the accompanying text that makes illustrations meaningful (cf. ibid. 295). Pictures focus on specific aspects of the words and have viewers interpret them. Therefore, a picture book contains three stories: the one told by words, the one implied by the pictures, and the one that results from a combination of the two. What happens if text and illustrations are different? When both parts conflict with each other, there is irony.

> **TIP**
>
> Look at your favorite childhood picture books again and see how text and pictures interact and which artistic and stylistic devices the artist uses. Evaluate them based on the information you have gained in this chapter.
> Observe a child when reading her/his favorite book. Find out what she/he especially likes about the book.
> Anticipate problems that might occur in an intermediate reading classroom (grades 7–9) if you use a picture book. Have counter arguments ready, for example the difference of picture books for small children and picture books for young adults (see recommendations in this chapter).

Comic books

Comic books consist of many cartoons which are single panels. "A comic strip is an illustrated story told in a series of frames or panels accompanied by dialogue as appropriate". (FOSTER in ZIPES 1: 334) Originally, comics were humorous and appeared as series in newspapers, where children and teenagers were the main readers.

Funny comic books

The first "comics" (with the exception of Egyptian tomb painting or the tapestry of Bayeux, which are said to be the forerunners), appeared in the mid-19th century in English and German magazines. WILHELM BUSCH's *Max und Moritz* (1865), showing the rough humor in the boys' rebelliousness, had a great influence on comic books. KASTEN ET AL. refer to the cartoon style as "simple, playful, unrealistic or exaggerated" and add that it is "particularly good for creating humor and satire" (157). This is true for some of the Walt Disney studio comics of the 50s and 60s, published in newspapers and in pulp magazines for younger age groups.

The first "comic books"

But in the 1930s, hero adventure stories used for serious purposes became longer, appeared in *Action Comics* (1938), and the style became more realistic and darker. The first superhero, "Superman" (1937), becomes almost a mythical, invincible figure, a good character fighting evil for the sake of the common man. In the 1960s, the previously popular morale-boosting Cold War superhero action comics starring Superman and Captain America became less popular in the USA. The superheroes were deconstructed. *Spider Man* (1963) became flawed and vulnerable, began to have problems with girls, for example. In the following two decades, comics became something like an insider genre. Only in the last two decades have they gained enormous popularity among young adults, who have become the main readers (FOSTER in ZIPES 1: 338; Collins in ZIPES 4: 59). Since the 1990s, comics have been dominated by co-operations with television shows, movies, and computer games; they are marketed with a vast amount of merchandise. *Star Wars* and *The Simpsons* are only two such examples.

Serious superhero action „comics"

Chapter 2 Young adult fiction for EFL learners

Graphic novels

From „comics" to serious graphic novels

The 2009 exhibition "Superman und Golem" at the Frankfurt Jewish Museum illustrates exactly the transition from the "comics genre" to the "graphic novel genre". The term "graphic novel" which was coined in 1978 by comic veteran WILL EISNER, refers to illustrated comic-style books with more serious themes, addressed at more mature audiences. The term "comic", which is still used, now refers to the style of the drawings and no longer to a funny content. EISNER applied the term in order to make his own work stand out against the superhero comic titles of his time, and later it was adopted by all kinds of book-length, high-quality, comic books that introduce readers to a wide range of literary fiction and non-fiction subjects. The term is also used to distinguish between comic books, usually published in series, and the longer graphic novels with a clear beginning, middle, and end (cf. PAWUK 2007; OSBORN 2001).

Jewish artists depicting immigration and the Holocaust

WILL EISNER and ART SPIEGELMAN, both Jewish-Americans started to use their cartoon art for stories that were not comic at all. In *The Contract with God Trilogy* (1976), EISNER combines autobiographical and historical elements to illustrate his and his family's Jewish-American assimilation process in New York. ART SPIEGELMAN created two *Maus* cartoons about his father's life in a concentration camp, in which Nazis are represented as cats and Jews as mice (the first volume was published in 1986), for which he received the Pulitzer Prize in 1992 (As early as 1955, AL FELDSTEIN & BERNARD KRIGSTEIN had already published *Master Race*, an encounter between survivor and torturer (cf. HOOG ET AL. 2008: 6)).

9/11 and other serious topics in graphic novel form

Since SPIEGELMAN's success, the genre has become widely accepted as a separate literary art form. *In The Shadow of No Towers*, SPIEGELMAN tells the story of how the collapse of the Twin Towers affected his life and that of his family in New York. Other cartoons have been created about the same theme, such as JACOBSEN's & COLON's *The 9/11 Report* (2006). HORNSCHEMEIER's psychologically insightful *Mother, Come Home*, a tale of a son trying to come to terms with his mother's cancer, was first published in graphic form in 2002. British cartoonist RAYMOND BRIGGS' *Gentleman Jim* is a socially critical attempt to present the life of a toilet man who wants to change jobs. After finally being imprisoned for various attempts to help himself and the poor, he finds time to complete "the levels" (O' and A' levels, terms he does not understand) which he needs to be able to get a new job.

The popularity of graphic novels for teens and adults

Nowadays, in the first decade of the new millennium, the genre is selling well. Every US public library has a graphic novel section, mostly in the juvenile section, but there is often one additional area in the adult department (cf. http://www.princetonlibrary.org). As a librarian and expert of the genre, PAWUK illustrates, in the introduction to his graphic novel guide, how and why libraries are promoting the graphic novel collection for pre-teens, teenagers, and adults (without page).

Graphic novels can comprise all kinds of subgenres, from fiction to non-fiction. The genre is generally broken down into books about superheroes, action and adventure, science fiction, fantasy, crime and mystery, horror, contemporary life, humor, and non-fiction, many of which overlap (cf. PAWUK VIIff.).

Recommendations for the secondary classroom
Grade 5–6

> For fifth grade beginners (or even earlier grades), *My Dad and My Mum* seem very appropriate. Not only is BROWNE's artwork with its surrealistic elements worth examining, but so is the interplay of artwork and text. The story of *My Dad*, consisting of only 22 pages, is ambiguous: it is funny and serious at the same time.
>
> The picture story is about a father who, from the viewpoint of a child, can do anything: he is not afraid, not even of the "Big Bad Wolf", he is strong; he is happy; he is big; he is soft; he is wise; he is a fast runner and swimmer, a great dancer, a brilliant singer, a fantastic footballer; but he is also "daft" and he makes the boy laugh. The poetic text that uses a lot of comparisons with similes (as –as, like) is mainly taken from the animals' world.
>
> It ends with: "I love my dad. And you know what? HE LOVES ME! And he always will." The sometimes surrealistic pictures tell a slightly different story: about a man in a checkered house coat and red slippers whose face does not always look happy. The book tells the story of a very ordinary man who is idolized by his small son. The father is simply very human and that is also expressed and emphasized in the pictures.
>
> BROWNE himself says in an interview: "I put in a lot of background to give another layer to the story. As a child I'd always liked cowboys and Indians stories where there were two layers – gruesome in the foreground but funny in the background. I used that as my model." (www.guardian.co.uk/books/2000/jul/29/booksforchildrenandteenagers)
>
> For fifth graders, it is probably wise to leave out the last picture (if the pictures are shown to the class) depicting a very small child in his father's arms, which might make the book look a bit childish for 10-year-olds.
>
> DUNCAN (2009), who says BROWNE's stories are full of "warmth, humanity and compassion" (44), suggests using symbols like the sun and the father's checkered dressing gown (that is repeated in every picture) and drawing a story board (57ff.). This requires a closer look at the pictures, where the sun is repeated in all shapes and sizes, but

ANTHONY BROWNE:
My Dad;
My Mum

cannot always be detected at first sight. Once, the sun is hidden on a stocking hanging from a washing line, and in the last picture it shines from under his dressing gown. The pictures make clear that Browne has been greatly inspired by surrealism, especially by Magritte. In bilingual art classes, this could very well be a topic in higher grades.

My Mum was done after the great success of *My Dad*. If children are to imitate Browne's book to write their own mother or father books, it is wise to let them choose one of the two.

MAURICE SENDAK: *Where the Wild Things Are* and other picture books

Although this story is about a very young, maybe kindergarten-age child, SENDAK's *Where the Wild Things Are* may be well used in the 5th grade. Without talking much about it, but by introducing a few key words, teachers can retell the story of "wild Max" with the help of the pictures. After that, children may learn (some of) the text by heart and retell it again or act it out in the classroom with the help of the pictures. KILPATRICK (1994) presents other useful ideas.

Any information about the story, its interpretation, or SENDAK's easily recognizable style may be provided in German. Perhaps children will find more books by one of the greatest living artists at home or in the local public library. Most of them are a delight to look at, to talk about, and to read (cf. KUSHNER 2003).

The Scholastic video collection, *Where the Wild Things Are... and other Maurice Sendak stories* (2002), can also be highly recommended. In addition to the animated pictures, the film music expressively underscores and interprets the story. Children could act out the story while using the silent film. Or they could write English or German subtitles.

Apart from learning the language, children will become motivated to read easy stories and develop a love of stories accompanied by artistic drawings. Some might rediscover their own childhood books; others will discover books that they may have missed out on. Some might have seen the children's opera, too, for which SENDAK himself wrote the libretto. Reading more of SENDAK's books in German (to be found in public libraries) is of course more than acceptable at this stage. However, teachers should have more English picture books in the class library, which should be started in fifth grade and continued throughout middle and high school.

Pierre, another small SENDAK volume, about the boy Pierre who keeps repeating "I don't care", can be recommended as the language repetitions will be learned rhythmically.

The above mentioned film collection also includes SENDAK's Caldecott Award winning title *In the Night Kitchen*.

KORKY PAUL & ROBIN TZANNES: *Professor Puffendorf's Secret Potion*

For sixth grade, the humorous books by ROBIN TZANNES & KORKY PAUL seem very suitable. *Professor Puffendorf's Secret Potion* has proven to be quite readable, funny, and good to work with in a 6th grade *Realschule* class (cf. KIST 2006). Learners can draw on their knowledge of the sorcerer's apprentice (*Der Zauberlehrling*), or if they do not know it, the German story could be a starting point.

The story is about Professor Puffendorf who leaves her apprentice Enzo alone in charge of her laboratory. Enzo steals the top secret potions and tries them out on a chipmunk. When he gives the last potion to Chip, the potion makes a dream come true: Chip wishes to be Enzo and thus Enzo gets imprisoned in Chip's cage. After that the professor and Chip party!

In contrast to BROWNE's art, these pictures are full of scraggly lines and forms, crowded with people, tubes, and glasses used in laboratories. The humor is evident at first sight in the funny artwork which distorts characters' faces and figures.

Other books like the *Winnie the Witch* series by VALERIE THOMAS & KORKY PAUL, published by Oxford University Press, are easily available in Germany through Cornelsen.

WILLIAM STEIG: *CDB!* and *CDC?*

WILLIAM STEIG's picture books are highly delightful, entertaining, humorous, and satirical stories for all ages. WILLIAM STEIG, who died in 2003 and whose work was exhibited in The Jewish Museums in New York (2007) and San Francisco (2008), was not only a children's author but is also known for his cartoons that appeared in *The New Yorker* magazine.

Although *CDB!* and *CDC?* do not contain continuous stories as each pictures speaks for itself, I recommend them here since pictures and letters/numbers complement each other.

After only a few months of English and some English alphabet reading training, STEIG's *CDB!* and *CDC?* can be deciphered and enjoyed easily. Readers have to read the acronyms out loud and connect the words that the letters stand for with the pictures. Deciphering the acronyms definitely promotes visual literary.

WILLIAM STEIG: *Doctor De Soto*

In the humorous fable *Doctor De Soto*, STEIG tells and illustrates the story of a mouse-dentist who is kind enough to treat all patients, except "cats and other dangerous animals". He makes one exception, however, and decides to treat a fox with a bad toothache who appears at his doorstep. As a fox, he is cunning: when he returns the next day to get his gold tooth replacement, he plans to devour the mouse. Luckily, Doctor De Soto and his wife, working as his assistant, have anticipated this and find a way to outfox the ungrateful fox.

Sixth-graders should have no trouble understanding the story since they can draw on their knowledge of pets and animal fables. With the clever and funny story, their vocabulary will expand and learning English will become highly entertaining!

WILLIAM STEIG's water-color art, with characters drawn in fine black lines, showing animals in human actions and in human attire, adds a lot to the humor of this popular fable about "underdogs" tricking superior beings.

An animated 10-minute film with the same title can be used as an addition to or a substitute for the picture book.

The same DVD titled *Pete's A Pizza and more William Steig stories* contains, in addition to STEIG's *Pete's A Pizza and The Amazing Bone*, TOMI UNGERER's *The Three Robbers* and MAGARET MAHY's *The Great Man Eating Shark* as well.

2 Picture books, comics and graphic novel

Grade 7–8

In 7th and 8th grades, JEFF SMITH's extremely successful Eisner award-winning comic series *Bone* should present a welcome change from the rather childish textbook illustrations. Each part of the series deals with the adventures of the three Bone cousins: brave Fone Bone, Phoney Bone, and easygoing Smiley Bone. They leave their home, Boneville, to encounter all kinds of fantasy creatures and evil forces out to conquer humankind.

An interesting and varied American teachers' guide is available online (http://www.scholastic.com/graphix/Scholastic_BoneDiscussion.pdf). The first two *Bone* video games were published in 2005 and 2006.

JEFF SMITH: BONE: Out of Boneville

In any higher grade, the playful, funny, entertaining collection of comics *It Was a Dark and Silly Night* edited by ART SPIEGELMAN, could be a highly motivating read. The story's title and the words "It was a dark and silly night…" were given to 13 well-known cartoonists and writers, who all made short 1–4-page stories from it. Among the artists are LEMONY SNICKET, NEIL GAIMAN, KAZ, and JOOST SWARTE. The last page, designed by R. SIKRYAK (48), is a guided tale of how to make one's own "dark and silly tale" leaving gaps for readers to fill in. The fourth story by TONY MILLIONAIRE is a page of 6 pictures appearing in the wrong order. The editors ask readers to put them into the correct order (18). Funny pictures of an owl's shopping trip at night form a puzzle. Learners are to verbalize their solutions.

Further recommendations include *Folklore & Fairy Tale Funnies* with fairy tales, old and retold, and *Big Fat Little Lit*, a collection compiled and edited by MOULY & SPIEGELMAN, with funny pictures drawn by a large variety of artists.

ART SPIEGELMAN & FRANCOISE MOULY: (Eds.): It Was a Dark and Silly Night

Grade 9–10

Very few people realize that the enormously popular film *Shrek* (2001) is based on STEIG's picture book *Shrek!* (1990). Shrek means "fear" in Yiddish. It is a fairytale parody of two "monsters" who fall in love with each other, "defying the fairytale notion that love is only for the young and beautiful" (NAHSON: 14). As in *Doctor De Soto*, the artist's empathy for the underdog is intense and genuine, which is one of the reasons why it may appeal to children. Shrek's imperfections make him the perfect modern hero because he is flawed.

Both the book's content and its art have been changed by the movie makers and this provides a good basis for comparison. In this case, the book should definitely be read before the film. The novel's exquisite and partly old-fashioned, fairytale-like language must be annotated for EFL learners, but since the text is rather short, it will prove a worthwhile task.

WILLIAM STEIG: Shrek!

Chapter 2   Young adult fiction for EFL learners

SHAUN TAN:
The Arrival

Since immigration to the US is often a theme in the upper grades of the *Mittelstufe*, the totally wordless, highly artistic picture story *The Arrival* by Australian SHAUN TAN, will definitely provide some challenging creative tasks for the EFL classroom after the class has dealt with basic immigration history in the 19th–early 20th centuries.

Learners could write their own speech bubbles, captions, or even whole stories to accompany the pictures. *The Arrival* is told in six chapters and contains realistic-looking black/brown and white pictures, inspired by realism, symbolism, and surrealism. One page may contain 12-30 small pictures or one large drawing may extend across two pages. The style is at times reminiscent of the 2008 Caldecott Medal winning graphic novel *The Invention of Hugo Cabret*, and at other times of Chagall's playful pictures or of Feininger's cubist paintings.

KAREN HESSE's *Letters from Rifka* and REILLY GIFF's *A House of Tailors* are good novels to acquire some basic background knowledge of the plight of immigrant children (see historical fiction chapter 2.5).

GENE LUEN YANG:
American Born Chinese

Another challenging graphic novel for the upper intermediate classroom is the Newbery award-winning coming-of-age story *American Born Chinese*, which tells the story of a Taiwanese-American immigrant who has a hard time growing up in a strange and sometimes xenophobic environment. He eats lunch by himself in a corner of the schoolyard, is bullied by "jocks" (students involved in school sports with privileged positions), and "has a crush" on a pretty classmate.

The graphic novel contains three plotlines: the efforts of the Chinese folk hero Monkey King who distances himself from his humble origins and is adored as a god; the struggles of Jin Wang, a lonely Asian-American middle school student who does everything to try to fit in; and the troubles of an All-American teen who is so ashamed of his Chinese cousin Chin-Kee that he has to change schools. At the end, these seemingly separate tales converge so that the stereotype of Chin-Kee is destroyed and both Jin Wang and the Monkey King are happy to be who they are.

Since the story was originally created for the web, the clear, concise lines and coloring make the style simple, yet expressive.

Boys' books – girls' books?

LELAND MYRICK:
Missouri Boy

Missouri Boy, another coming of age story, is the memoir of a white boy's transition from childhood to adulthood, represented by the setting: he spends his childhood in Missouri, and a trip to California represents the transition to adulthood. Fourth of July with firecrackers in a tree in the yard; skinny-dipping in a pond in the woods; first attempts at romance; these events are all only part of the memoir. Childhood is depicted as both simple and complex, more complex of course when he has to witness his brother's imprisonment. There is minimal dialogue and few lyrical captions, making each section a visual poem. The block colors and rough outlines of MYRICK's art suggest an unsentimental kind of nostalgia for the writer's own youth.

Girls should read WEINSTEIN's semi-autobiographical *Girl Stories*, an account of the author's own experience of the eighth and ninth grades. The short, bitter, but also hilarious stories depict her being greatly worried about all kinds of teenage girls' problems: naval piercing, extreme concern with her reputation, (since she still plays with Barbie dolls), anger at being Jewish at Christmas time, and confusion about the opposite sex. Weinstein's drawings consist of scraggly lines and bright neon colors, which could be taken from a teenage cosmetics case.

LAUREN WEINSTEIN: *Girl Stories*

Reluctant readers

The *House that Crack Built* is about anti-supermen and anti-heroes; it is about consumers, traders, and dealers of crack.

The title and the text of the story told in verse are based on the old English nursery rhyme "This is the House that Jack Built." As the rhyme is not part of young Germans' general knowledge, it might be wise to have learners first listen to or read the traditional rhyme dealing with Jack's house. *The House that Crack Built* uses the same rhythm starting with a main clause and a relative clause, with one more relative clause being added on in each verse. It starts like this: "This is the House that crack built." Second page: "This is the Man who lives in the House that crack built." Third page: "These are Soldiers who guard the Man who lives in the House that crack built."

In verse connected by the relative pronoun "who" (instead of "that" of the original), the story tells of the relationship between young male and female drug users, their offspring, street dealers, and gangs. In very few words, it also includes poor Central and South American farmers whose subsistence depends on the drug trade. JAN THOMPSON DICKS' art seems influenced by Mexican folk art, with its stark colors and partly folk, partly expressionist style that conveys the drug business' cruelty. The cruelty is especially emphasized in the last picture where a baby is lying half-naked on a green blanket with no protection. Each framed page on the right side is accompanied by the verse on the left. The pictures are very stark and expressive.

CLARK TAYLOR & JAN THOMPSON DICKS: *The House that Crack Built*

For more books for reluctant readers turn to chapter 2.10.

> **TIP**
> *Research other established and younger artists' work for children. Buy yourself "Big Fat Little Lit" and see for yourself how different the art work and the texts are.*
> *Research more of Scholastic's and other international publishers' efforts to present more motivating material to improve young people's literacy. Compare it to German publishers' materials.*

3 Problem novels

Realism

In the following chapter I will present various types of young adult literature, the first dealing with realistic fiction. The events described in "realistic fiction" could actually occur or have occurred to people or animals in real life. Characters in realistic novels react to situations in the same way real people might react. The genre is sometimes divided into factual, situational, emotional, and social realism. In factual realism, facts describing actual persons, places, and events are accurately recorded; this is often a main characteristic of historical fiction. In "situational realism", a situation is not only possible, but probable. The author identifies both location and characters by place, age, and social class and treats them in a believable manner. The survival story is an example of this type of realism. "Emotional realism", often a major element in the coming-of-age story, depicts believable feelings and relationships among characters. "Social realism" provides an honest portrait of society, of both good and bad elements. In realistic fiction some or all of these categories are often combined. (Cf. CONTINUUM ENCYCLOPEDIA OF CHILDREN'S LITERATURE ONLINE).

Realistic fiction often comprises socially critical literature and the problem novel, in which issues of everyday life – in individual lives and in societies or even the whole world – are addressed. Problems like bullying, friendships, family affairs, and sexuality play an important role as well as political and ecological problems, for example racism and war (cf. JOOSEN in ZIPES 3: 328).

Didacticism in problem novels

Since the "revolutionary 1960s", realism in YA literature has played an important role. Authors used real events in social situations in order to teach children how to behave "politically correctly". This time period was characterized by didactic novels in which the readers were to be taught how to act. In this respect, these novels were not so different from the didactic literature of the beginnings of children's literature in the 18th century.

But the problem novels were the first to create a separate children's and YA market, which had not existed in such a form before. The publication of *The Catcher in the Rye* (1951) is often considered a benchmark, although Salinger did not intend it to be a YA novel. Nonetheless, with its depiction of a troubled adolescent who does not really want to grow up, it is often seen as one of the first "problem novels" for young adults. The 1967 publication of *The Outsiders* by 15-year-old S.E Hinton is considered another stepping stone in the establishment of the YA market (cf. MARQUI in ZIPES 2: 232). US writers like PAUL ZINDEL and JUDY BLUME depicted real issues and problems that youngsters might encounter, one of them being sexuality, which until BLUME's publication of *Then Again, Maybe I Won't* (1971) and *Forever* (1975) had not been touched upon. Today there are almost no taboos left in YA literature. Any problems children might face – violence, sex and love in hetero- and homosexual relationships, rape, child abuse, illness and handicaps, life in the streets – may be dealt with in current YA literature (cf. HESSE 2002a: 22f.). Nowadays, novels are less didactic than in the 1970s. Instead, they are meant to help young people cope with their developmental tasks (cf. BUSHMAN & PARKS 2003; NISSEN 1988, see chapter 1).

Recommendations for the secondary classroom
Grade 5–6
For younger learners of English, picture books dealing with children's real life may be appropriate. Family stories, school stories, and animal stories exist in abundance. However, I would really not start with problem novels in the first two grades of secondary school but would use funny stories instead (see chapter 2.2). If a teachers wants to deal with death, maybe due to an event that has shattered the class, English poet MICHAEL ROSEN's *Sad* can be recommended.

> ROSEN's & BLAKE's *Sad* is a heart–rending story about the death of the author's son. Pictures and text complement each other very well. Here the relationship between design (colors, lines etc.) and content becomes clear. It may be a good choice for a class library.

MICHAEL ROSEN & QUENTIN BLAKE: *Sad*

Grade 7–8

> Set in Florida, *The Tiger Rising* is a relatively short tale of 12-year-old Rob who finds a caged tiger in the woods behind the motel where he lives with his dad. The tiger is so strange in this setting that Rob sees it as some kind of magic trick. The owner of the motel gives him the task to feed the creature and Rob notices a similarity between himself and the tiger, since he has locked all his feelings inside a kind of cage. But the tiger also takes his mind away from his mourning.
> With the help of Sistine, an independent city girl, he develops a new relationship with his father, which slowly takes his mind off his sadness. Quotes from WILLIAM BLAKE's "The Tiger" set the tone.
> The short novel deals not only with death, grief, and sadness, but it also becomes a suspenseful adventure story when the tiger appears on the scene and no one knows where he came from.

KATE DICAMILLO: *The Tiger Rising*

Chapter 2   Young adult fiction for EFL learners

Grade 8–9

ROBERT SWINDELLS: *Abomination*

Thirteen-year-old Martha is bullied at school. She is not allowed to do anything other children her age do since her parents are very strict, old-fashioned religious fundamentalists. She is an outsider at school until she meets a new student, a boy, whom she slowly befriends. When she takes him to her house one day, he hears screams from inside the house. Martha has to keep a terrible secret, but with the help of her new boyfriend Scott, she is able to share it and together they free the small, illegitimate child that had been held captive in the cellar for five years. The suspenseful novel is driven by the reader's wish to know what or who "Abomination" is. To know that the word abomination means "Ekel" in German does not really help to understand what it is. One has to read it, relatively quickly!

TERRY TRUEMAN: *Inside Out*

When two teenage brothers attempt to hold up a Spokane coffee shop where Zach, 16, is waiting for his mother to bring his antipsychotic medicine, a hostage drama begins. Zach, who suffers from schizophrenia (he hears voices in his head and has trouble understanding reality), tells the story of the two desperate young gangsters who are awaited by the police outside. When the other hostages are released, Zach volunteers to remain the only hostage. An odd bonding follows between the two robbers – actually rather nice teens – and Zach. The old guns that they threaten their hostages with do not function any more and the reason they hold up the shop is because their mother has cancer and needs money for her treatments. When the brothers surrender, Zach is reunited with his mother who brings his badly needed medicine. A teacher's guide is available for this suspenseful small novel. It can also be read as a mystery story.

Grade 9–10

BERLIE DOHERTY: *Dear Nobody*

Although the theme is teenage pregnancy, this epistolary novel, written from both male and female points of view – is not really about sex, but about the development of the two main characters Chris and Helen after having had sex for the first time.

The pregnancy leads Helen to a new understanding of her parents and grandparents and thus to a new and closer connection to the previous generations. Although the two lovers do not mature enough to found a family, they are both overwhelmed by their happiness about baby Amy's birth at the end (cf. HESSE & PUTJENTER 2001). The novel has been turned into a play (cf. CollinsEducational 1995) and a BBC film consisting of three parts (available through Klett).

3 Problem novels

Boys' book – girls' books

Dear Nobody is not a girls' book, although Helen has the more important part. One could, however, use this sensitive novel and divide up the easily separable two points of view and have males read Chris' narrative part and girls read Helen's "Dear Nobody" letters to the newborn baby.

ANGELA JOHNSON's *The First Part Last*, a teen pregnancy story told from the perspective of a 16-year-old New York graffiti sprayer, may be considered a boys' book. At least the male perspective is the only one since his girlfriend is in the hospital and has no active part in the story. It can be assumed, however, that both genders will be interested in the sensitively told story.

Most of WALTER DEAN MYERS' books for young adults can be read as problem novels for males, e.g. *Monster*, which deals with a black male's life in prison. Parts of it can be acted out very well.

Reluctant readers (Grade 8–10)

Todd Strasser: *Give a Boy a Gun*

This multi-perspective, full-sized novel is good for reluctant readers because not every student has to read the whole book, which consists of many voices narrating the same event: Gary and Brendan, two high school students, take the whole school community hostage. It ends in the suicide of one and a life-threatening injury of the other. Friends, enemies, parents, teachers and counselors are involved and all tell the story from their perspectives.

Each student could choose and read one of the many characters' views and try to understand "his/her" character in relation to the two protagonists. They all ask themselves which role they played in the tragedy. This could also be played in readers' theater, with everybody appearing in their role and defending their views. An amateur film made from a performance of *Give a Boy a Gun* at the Pädagogische Hochschule Freiburg (2007) could be watched at the end.

MARYBETH LORBIECKI & DAVID DIAZ: *Just One Flick of a Finger*

This picture book, drawn in the style of Mexican graffiti artists, deals with the danger of carrying and owning a gun. The protagonist is called bad names, thinks of revenge, steals his father's gun, takes his gun to school, is again bullied at school, his friend (whose brother is serving time in jail for using a gun) wants to prevent him from shooting, the gun goes off, and he and his friend find themselves badly wounded in hospital. The protagonist donates blood to his friend and both are saved.

On the left-hand side, one-page pictures, similar to *The House that Crack Built*, with black frames correspond with the text. The short text is written in verse. Some vocabulary should be annotated.

Chapter 2 Young adult fiction for EFL learners

> **TIP**
>
> Reflect on the advantages and disadvantages of problem novels in class. Read Laura Halse Anderson's "Speak", a highly praised, award-winning realistic novel about high school rape. Would you use it in the classroom? Discuss the limits of realistic fiction.
> Teenage pregnancy is a popular theme in YA fiction (cf. The ALAN Review). Read the two novels recommended above and analyze their narrative perspective. Decide which one you would choose for your learners.

4 Multicultural novels

Definition

The multicultural novel genre focuses on "the social realities of cultural groups, based on ethnic, religious, or national heritage. What the culture is, in relation to traditions, beliefs and worldview, plays a significant part in the work. Often the cultural group is under-represented and unassimilated" (WATSON 2001: 497). The term 'multicultural' usually means 'multi-ethnic', but it can also mean 'cross-cultural' referring to the status of its protagonists as immigrants, refugees, and travelers. It refers to "literature written by and about minorities, by and about immigrants ..., and by those from other countries who write about the adolescent experience in other lands" (HAYN & SHERRILL 1996). HAYN's & SHERRILL's statement that it is literature about immigrants "recently assimilated into this culture", (http://scholar.lib.vt.edu/ejournals/ALAN/fall96/f96-09-Hayn.html Mar 26, 2008) seems incorrect since the literature often deals with just the opposite, namely with incomplete or unsuccessful assimilation and the problems of integration.

In multicultural novels, experiences of alienation are often reflected, for example:
- Experiences of native Americans: *The Absolutely True Diary of a Part-Time Indian; Code Talker*
- Experiences of African Americans: *Locomotion; Monster; The First Part Last*
- Alienation of strangers in a strange land, e.g. Latinos: *The Circuit, Breaking Through*; or of Asians: *Dragonwings, Children of The River; Kim/Kimi; Kira-Kira, Journey to Topaz*
- Life of Indian-English youths in Great Britain: *(Un)arranged Marriage*
- Problems of immigration: *Crossing the Wire; La Línea, Abela*
- Problems of young migrants living in their own country: *Abela, La Línea, Homeless Bird*
- Living as "illegals" in a strange land: *Abela, La Línea*

Growing importance of multicultural novels

With a growing awareness of people living in Western multicultural societies, the ethnic youth novel has received increasing attention in recent years, not only for the general book market but also for the EFL classroom (cf. BURWITZ-MELZER 2003; HESSE 2002 c, d; 2009b; MUKHERJEE 2006; MÜLLER-HARTMAN & RICHTER 2002a, b).

4 Multicultural novels

All authors agree that it is important to offer teenagers of migrant families literature depicting youths whose protagonists they may identify with, whose problems and ideas they can understand more easily. Told from teen perspectives, the stories offer an especially good opportunity for teenage readers to empathize with the young protagonists.

Recommendations for the secondary classroom
Grade 5–6

> *The Great Migration* with paintings and wood carvings by the famous African-American artist JACOB LAWRENCE uses just a few words to tell the story of the great migration of blacks from the South to the North.

JACOB LAWRENCE: *The Great Migration*

> *Harriet and the Promised Land* narrates the life of Harriet Tubman, the former slave who helped other slaves to escape to the North.
> The pictures, done in bold colors and woodcarvings, are accompanied by a sparse rhythmic text. They are full of urgency and movement; Harriet looks like a protective angel; her huge, brown hand is like the spreading roots and branches of the trees. The North Star is always shining. In word and image, Lawrence shows and tells how stories can inspire (cf. ROCHMAN at amazon.com).

JACOB LAWRENCE: *Harriet and the Promised Land*

> The small book for native primary-age children may be a good story for 5th and 6th grade EFL learners (cf. SENF ET AL. 2008). In its 48 illustrated pages, it tells the story of two children from different cultural backgrounds, one from Mexico and one from the USA, whose common love and "language of communication" are soccer.

JEAN MARZOLLO & BLANCHE SIMS: *Soccer Sam*

Grade 7–8

> Both *La Línea* and *Crossing the Wire* can be read starting at the end of 8th grade (cf. KIST 2009). These exciting novels are about the attempts of children to cross the Mexican border to get to their parents, who have been living across "la línea" for a long time.
> The advantage of *La Línea* is that an annotated version and a teacher's guide exist (cf. KIST 2009), but *Crossing the Wire* is equally suspenseful. Ann Jaramillo herself teaches migrant middle school students in California and says she wanted to write a story that especially these children can relate to (cf. HESSE 2008).

ANN JARAMILLO: *La Línea* and WILLIAM HOBBS: *Crossing the Wire*

Grade 9–10

Bali Rai: (Un)arranged Marriage

This is another novel about an Indian youngster who has never seen India. He was born in multicultural Leicester/England and has multicultural friends. But his parents and older brothers want him to become a good Punjabi man. On his 13th birthday, his father announces that he will marry an Indian girl on his 17th birthday. In the following four years, Manny pulls all kinds of pranks and commits petty crimes to make himself unattractive to his future in-laws. When, on a family vacation in Punjab, he is left in India to be straightened out, he plans revenge on his family: to "un-arrange" his marriage.

The teacher's guide (BÖGEL & HESSE 2008) shows that the novel can be taught in both the *Mittelstufe* (grade 9–10) and in the *Oberstufe* (grades 11–12). An amateur DVD of the Pädagogische Hochschule Freiburg stage production (2008) can be watched for post-reading.

Paul Fleischman: Seedfolks

Seedfolks deals with multiculturalism in a kind of parable, in which 13 multi-ethnic members of a run-down neighborhood in Cleveland are portrayed. They occupy a vacant lot and build a community garden, one of the many inner-city gardens that exist in big US cities. Each of the 13 stories tells something about the characters' past and present lives and how they connect through the garden. The small book is not as easy as one might think so it also works well in 11th grade (cf. HESSE 2002c).

Boys' book – girls' books

Gloria Wheelan: Homeless Bird

Homeless Bird tells the fairy tale-like story of the 12-year-old bride Koly who is married off into the family of a sickly, equally young husband. The in-laws want to get the dowry so that they can buy the boy's badly needed medicine. When he and Koly's friendly father-in-law die, the young girl is left to the mercy of her mean mother-in-law. She has to fend for herself when she is left alone in the holy city of Vrindavan, the widow city of India. There she can use her embroidery skills, which are finally discovered by a wealthy sponsor. She is also able to find a gentle young husband who is enlightened enough to marry a widow. The insightful novel seems more appropriate for girls.

Narinder Dhami: Bend it Like Beckham

One of the few books with female protagonists that appears to attract both boys and girls is *Bend it like Beckham*, which was written for teenagers after the film with the same title. Gifted Indian-English soccer player Jesminder (Jess) wants to play soccer in London like some of her English friends. After a lot of obstacles, she is finally able to persuade her parents to let her play professional football. The annotated version (2004) allows readers to read it quickly. A teacher's guide (cf. SPIELER 2006) makes teaching easier. (For classroom research based on this novel see JÄGER 2009).

Reluctant readers

Much to the disapproval of his parents, Baljit is mad about football and when he is invited to trials at Leicester City, he has to lie about his whereabouts. Unlike Manjit in *(Un)arranged Marriage*, Bajit is part of a warm and witty family. Other issues the small novel deals with, besides growing up, are prejudice and friendship.
Other appropriate multicultural books for reluctant readers are *One Flick of a Finger* (see chapter 2.3 and *The House that Crack Built* (see chapter 2.2).

BALI RAI:
Dream On

> **TIP**
> *Watch some of the films for your own enrichment:*
> ▶ ***Indian-English issues:** "Fond Kiss, A"*
> ▶ *"Bend it Like Beckham"*
> ▶ *The amateur film of (Un)arranged Marriage;*
>   *(to be used in the intermediate classroom)*
> ▶ *"Water": **Indian girls as widows***
> ▶ ***Migration from South and Central America to the US:** "Maria Full of Grace".*
>   *There are also various documentaries on crossing the Mexican-American border (e.g. Wetback).*

5 Historical fiction

Historical fiction depicts stories set in the past which attempt, with the aid of the author's scholarly research, "to reconstruct and bring life to events, culture and *Zeitgeist* of the period" (WATSON 2001: 334). Children's writers emphasize not so much major events in history, but the lives of the young characters who lived through that time. Today's historical children's and teen novels usually show what it was like for ordinary characters to live during a certain period. Factual, situational, and social elements are the basis for writers of historical fiction in which the hardships, the adventures, and the experiences of the young protagonists can be felt.

Definition

Since the 1980s, the genre has grown in popularity, after its neglect in the 1960s and the discussion about politically correct writing for children in the 70s. JILL PATON WALSH, author of *Parcel of Patterns*, a story about

Growing popularity

the bubonic plague in the small Derbyshire village of Eyam, hints at the past debates when she says "with a fervour reminiscent of Christian didacts of the 19th century, some people think it wrong to portray the world as it is or it was, and believe instead it should be only shown as it ought to be, sanitising reality in order to change it" (HUNT 1995: 302).

Current historical fiction

Today's writers of historical fiction point out that the historical novel is much more a faithful creation of minds and motives than a costume drama or an authentic recount of the time. Writers of historical fiction stress the careful study of time, landscape and location, social conditions, and language. But WALSH also admits that the point of view also depends on the time in which the literature is written (cf. HARRISON & MAGUIRE 1987: 268).

Placing familiar things into an unfamiliar context allows readers to see them and to see themselves afresh and thus expand their imagination. Historical fiction is like science fiction in reverse: "you take a historical problem out of context to observe it better; you have the reality of the past to latch on to" (HUNT 1995: 297).

Historical fiction for intercultural learning: then and now; you and me

With the advantages of historical fiction, teachers who often complain about their students' lack of interest in history, can take advantage of historical fiction as a bridge to understand the target culture and to foster intercultural learning. The genre comprises two levels: the level of then-and-now and that of you-and-I (members of two different cultures).

Historical fiction allows young learners to get involved in young people's lives of the past since they usually empathize with characters of their own age. Therefore, studying Northern Irish history, for example, a topic covered by every textbook on the German educational market, with a teenage novel like *Torn Away*, can bring forth outstanding results (HESSE 2002a).

US history in the YA *Dear America* series

From 1996–2004 the *Dear America* series for American teenagers was published to give children better access to their own history. All of the novels are written in diary form, in order to make readers feel what is was like for children of their age to live in the past. Events from the beginning of American history through the Vietnam War are depicted vividly in the series. It was stopped in 2004, but it inspired a nine-episode TV series on the pay-TV channel HBO.

For more advanced, sophisticated readers, a large variety of independent, non-serialized novels exist, which would make it a worthwhile project to study American literature on the basis of these novels. The following suggestions are only one possibility out of many:

5 Historical fiction

> **Indians in pre-colonial America:** *To Spoil the Sun*
>
> **Early settlement and persecution of witches:** *The Witch at Blackbird Pond, Witch Child*; **Before the founding of the United States:** *The Winter People*
> **Early USA:** *Fever 1793*
> **Westward expansion:** *The Captain's Dog: My Journey with the Lewis and Clark Tribe*
> **Expulsion of Cherokee-Indians in 1838:** *The Trail of Tears; Soft Rain*
> **Pioneer times:** *Little House in the Big Woods* (series); *Pioneer Cat, Save Queen of Sheba; The Birchbank House; Beyond the Great Divide*
> **Gold Rush:** *The Journal of Wong Ming-Chung; Gold Rush Winter*
> **Immigration 19th/20th century:** *Letters from Rifka; Bound for America; A Tree Grows in Brooklyn; A House of Tailors*
> **Industrialization:** *Lyddie*
> **Civil War:** *Bull Run; Soldier's Heart; A Light in the Storm*
> **Slavery and freedom for slaves:** *Day of Tears*
> **Late 19th century immigration to the US from Germany:** *A House of Tailors; How to Become an American*
> **Racism in Vermont in the 1920s:** *Witness*
> **Racism in the south in the 1930s:** *Roll of Thunder Hear My Cry*
> **WWI und settlement of the West:** *Hattie Big Sky; After the Dancing Days*
> **The Great Depression of the 1930s:** *Out of the Dust*
> **WWII, the Holocaust, and Japanese Relocation camps:** *Summer of My German Soldier; Journey to Topaz; Code Talker; Alan and Naomi*
> **Civil Rights Movement:** *The Watsons Go to Birmingham – 1963*
> **Vietnam War:** *Where Have All the Flowers Gone? The Diary of Molly MacKenzie Flaherty*
> **First Iraq War:** *Gulf*
> **Second Iraq War:** *Sunrise over Fallujah*
> **Mexicans fleeing to the USA:** *La Línea: Crossing the Wire*
> **Mexican migrants in the USA in the 1930s and today:** *Esperanza Rising: The Circuit*

US history through teenage fiction

Recommendations for the secondary classroom

Since historical and cultural information is generally not a main focus in the first few years of secondary school, I suggest books only in two categories: grades 6–7 and 8–10.

Chapter 2 Young adult fiction for EFL learners

Grade 6–7

William J. Hooks & Charles Robinson: *Pioneer Cat*

One of the many stories about American pioneer times is *Pioneer Cat*. On the way from Missouri to Oregon on a wagon train, Purdy is worried about her cat that she found in St. Joseph but was not allowed to take with her. She has to keep it a secret and tells her parents only after they have finally arrived in Oregon.

The tale includes accounts of the dangerous pioneer life on the Oregon Trail such as a buffalo stampede, river crossings, and encounters with not-so-friendly Indians.

Eve Bunting: *Dandelions*

This relatively long picture book gives a lively account of a pioneer family settling the West. The book is a somewhat fictionalized story of the hardships and worries of a pioneer family on the long way to the West. It is told from the point of view of one of the two girls in the family who is so sensitive that she realizes her parents' hidden conflict in the West. While her father is more pragmatic and tries to deal with the new situation in lonely Nebraska actively, her mother is homesick for Illinois. But the girl knows how to make her mother happy and contributes to making her feel at home by planting dandelions on their claim.

John Bruchac & Diana Magnuson: *Trail of Tears*

In only 48 illustrated pages, this book recounts the 1838 bloody expulsion of the Cherokees from their homeland in the southeastern USA and their route to a new settlement in Oklahoma, west of the Mississippi. This terrible 1200-mile-journey is known today as the Trail of Tears.

Bruchac himself is Indian and has written other Native American YA fiction and non-fiction.

Grade 8–10

Germans seen through foreign eyes

The novels recommended here are mostly immigrant stories, highly suitable for intercultural learning. Both *Summer of My German Soldier* and *Silver Days* (and its sequels) deal with Germans coming to America in the 1940s. They successfully mirror the anti-German sentiments from an American perspective. Magorian's *Good Night Uncle Tom*, written from the English perspective, should be equally well-suited for the German classroom. The novel is accompanied by a good film, but it is a bit long for intermediate learners.

5 Historical fiction

KAREN HESSE:
Letters from Rifka

This novel – written in letter form interspersed with Pushkin poems- tells the story of 12-year-old Rifka who, with her family, has to flee the anti-Semitism of post-revolutionary Russia in 1919 to emigrate to the USA. The letters tell of the fears and uncertainties of young Rifka, who has to be left behind in Belgium by her family for several months due to a bad ringworm infection.

When she is finally allowed to travel, she successfully reaches Ellis Island, but is taken into quarantine again because the ringworm infection left her bald and thus made her an undesirable immigrant. Eventually, however, Rifka manages to get permission to enter the country, proving that she will not become a ward of the state.

BETTY GREENE:
Summer of My German Soldier

German students might have studied anti-Semitism and WWII from the German point of view, but studying it through American fiction might give them a totally new perspective.

The award-winning *Summer of My German Soldier* covers the 1940s before the end of WWII. It mainly deals with the relationship of a young Jewish-American girl to a German prisoner of war (POW) whom she meets accidentally in her parents' store in small-town Arkansas. She develops a "crush" on this soldier who lives in a nearby camp. When he escapes from the camp, she secretly hides him in her parents' remote guest house. The only person she confides her secret to is the black maid, the only likable figure in the book apart from the two young protagonists. The German POW leaves, is shot, and she is found guilty of hiding an alien enemy, which leads to her arrest.

The story gives insight into the numerous WWII POW camps in rural USA, the way Germans were regarded and treated in war times, and how "collaborators" were charged. It also shows the widespread racial hatred and segregation in the USA of the 1940s. In connection with the film with the same title, it is highly recommended for intercultural projects (e.g. German-American email correspondence).

SONIA LEVITIN:
Silver Days

As Jewish emigrants from Nazi Germany, the Platts have to deal with a harsh, poor immigrant life in New York City in 1940. Both parents find only low paying, menial jobs to make ends meet for their family of five. When they move to California they have to start from scratch, but soon it becomes apparent that the three girls are so talented that they are accepted and advance in their schools very quickly. While the girls begin to be Americanized without noticing it (shaving their legs, experimenting with makeup, going to the movies etc.), their mother is still very much connected to Germany, especially because she had to leave her old mother behind. When she is informed about her mother's death in Auschwitz, she develops severe depression, from which she

Chapter 2   Young adult fiction for EFL learners

> recovers only slowly at the end when she is asked to take care of a newborn baby. Lisa, the middle daughter, tells the story of their life from 1940–1943 conveying the strength and spirit that helps them to survive.
>
> The book successfully shows the difference between the picture that the girls formed in their minds about America and the real life of immigrants in New York City and later in California. It mirrors the humiliation that Germans must have felt when they came from a relatively stable middle-class home and had to do the most inferior jobs. It also shows how much the Jewish-German ethics of hard, honest work and the aspirations the parents had for their girls helped them to make something of their lives.
>
> The novel mirrors the hope of immigrants during F. D. Roosevelt's government concerning the fight against Hitler. It also reflects how German-speaking immigrants were discriminated against, although they were patriotic and volunteered to fight for America in the war; later, after Pearl Harbor, it was the Japanese who were discriminated against.

YOSHIKO UCHIDA:
Journey to Topaz

> *Journey to Topaz* deals with these anti-Japanese sentiments which, after the attack on Pearl Harbor, led to evacuating Japanese and placing them in prison camps throughout the West. Topaz is the name of the prison camp in the Utah desert where Yuki and her family have to spend part of the war years.
>
> The 2005 Newbery Medal winner *Kira-kira* by Cynthia Kadohata presents the plight of poor Japanese in the post-WWII years.

Boys' books – girls' books?

Difference between female and male protagonists

All historical novels can be taught in coeducational settings. However, the books with female protagonists often do not only show the events, but also the insights and thoughts of the heroines, whereas books with male protagonists frequently narrate events and describe battles in which military strategies and weapons play an important role. That is why I recommend PAULSEN's *Soldier's Heart* for classes with predominantly male students and *Out of the Dust* more for females, although both novels are also appropriate for coeducational classes.

Civil War
GARY PAULSEN:
Soldier's Heart

> *Soldier's Heart* is the story of Charley Goddard's enlistment and Civil War experiences. Like many young men in Europe in WWI, Charles is eager to enlist with the first Minnesota volunteers in spite of his young age (15) since he expects the Civil War to be an exciting adventure. In the end, however, he has to find out that the war was nothing but physical and mental horror. Unlike many of his fellow soldiers, he

survives and comes home with a "soldier's heart". Another very impressive book about the Civil War is PAUL FLEISCHMAN's *Bull Run*.

Reluctant readers

Male reluctant readers may be most interested in stories of discoveries, explorations, battles, and wars. Using picture books and comics about heroes and explorers might motivate them to read. Also, pictures books about important historical explorations like the Lewis and Clark expedition, in which tools, machinery, and weapons play an important role, might catch their interest (see chapter 15.3). Films about historical events might also trigger reading.

> **TIP** *In WWII Germans and Japanese immigrants to the USA shared similar fates. After Pearl Harbor there were strong anti-Japanese sentiments, too. Compare and contrast German-Americans and Japanese-Americans in YA fiction and film. Watch the films "Summer of My German Soldier" and "Come See the Paradise".*

6 Adventure, animal and survival fiction

Adventure stories are stories about actions and events involving danger and conflict, developing with speed and urgency (WATSON 6). Adventure stories' protagonists live similar lives to the ones of fairy tales: the hero leaves home to meet a challenge, fights against an evil force, and returns home an even stronger hero.
Realistic adventure stories dominated the juvenile literature market during the twentieth century and are still a vibrant part of it today. Obviously, both historical and contemporary stories of adventure and survival have a powerful appeal for adolescents as they seem to prepare them for their own journeys toward independence.

Definition

What makes a current adventure story realistic is that it is usually set in a real setting and the protagonist is often a teenager from a rather poor or disadvantaged family. These teenagers have enough energy and commitment that allow them to fight for a good cause or against an evil force. Evil may appear in the form of wars, terrorist attacks, racism, greed, or even illnesses (*The Other Side of Truth*, *Abela*), extermination of certain animal species (*The Last Lobo*, *Thunder Cave* etc.). A good cause may be human rights, protection of the environment etc., in which teenager's morality plays a big role.

Realistic adventure stories

Chapter 2   Young adult fiction for EFL learners

Example: *Hoot*

For example, in HIAASON's environmentally engaged adventure story *Hoot*, three committed, smart and brave, partly bullied teenagers fight against a restaurant chain that is planning to build on a lot under which endangered miniature owls live in burrows. Roy, who has recently moved to Florida, befriends the homeless boy nicknamed Mullet Fingers and takes up his cause with the runaway's stepsister Beatrice. The DVD *Hoot* can be used as a lively interpretation of the story.

Survival stories

Survival is an important theme in many realistic American adventure stories. The vast, uninhabited wilderness often makes it hard for protagonists to survive. But with their natural wits, their extraordinary senses, their will to learn, and of course, with the help of friendly people and animals, young protagonists learn to overcome the dangers.

Examples of contemporary animal adventure and survival stories

PAULSEN's *Hatchet* with its sequels is a survival story set in the present. The novel is about a young boy stranded alone in the Canadian wilderness. After his plane crashes, Brian survives for 54 days with only a hatchet, a gift from his recently divorced mother. The Canadian wilderness is also the setting of HOBBS' *Far North*, in which a 15-year-old boy, his Indian boarding school roommate, and an elderly Native American find themselves stranded. In addition to *Julie of the Wolves*, a survival novel set in Alaska, GEORGE, a female writer of survival stories, also shows her commitment to the animal survival story elsewhere. In *My Side of the Mountain*, a boy can live through a dire food shortage with the help of a falcon he has trained himself. SMITH's main focus is on animal adventure: *Thunder Cave* is an exciting story about elephant smuggling in Kenya and *The Last Lobo*, focuses on saving endangered red wolves in the USA. The protection of elephants is also the theme in GILLIAN CROSS's *The Great Elephant Chase*.

In most cases where survival and animal adventure stories are combined, an intimate relationship between animals and humans evolves.

Recommendations for the secondary classroom

Examples of classical adventure stories (simplified)

Since many novels mentioned previously under different categories can also be read as adventure stories, (picture books and graphic novels, problem novels, historical fiction etc.) and since, especially today, many adventure books are fantasy (chapter 2,8), I will point here to the easy availability of simplified classical adventure novels. Such novels include LONDON's *Call of the Wild*, STEVENSON's *Treasure Island*, DEFOE's *Robinson Crusoe* or TWAIN's *The Adventures of Tom Sawyer & The Adventures of Huckleberry Finn*, some of which are accompanied by tasks and audio CDs.

> HELEN FROST's award-winning *Diamond Willow (2008)* tells the story of Willow, an Alaskan girl, who saves her dog from being killed in a wild sled ride to her grandparents' house. The story, written in relatively easy verse, blends exciting survival adventure with a contemporary girl's discovery of family roots and family secrets. The poems are shaped in a variety of diamonds in between which the prose narrative from the dog's point of view gives additional information.

HELEN FROST: *Diamond Willow*

Although a girl is the protagonist, I imagine boys will be interested in the story as well since it is an adventure story. The same should be true for GEORGE's *Julie of the Wolves*, also set in Alaska. Here Julie has to come to terms with wolves; she has to learn to read their behavior in order to be accepted by a pack of wolves, who help her to survive in the Arctic cold.

> *Look at the fantasy chapter and make a list of fantasy adventure stories. In how far does the adventure story apply to the fantasy genre too? Which are the qualities of a fantasy hero?*

7 Mystery: crime and detective novels

Mysteries cut across every genre, realistic and fantastic, contemporary and historical, but here I want to focus on realistic mystery and detective fiction, in which children and teenagers usually expose criminals, either alone or in small groups. Their superiority to adults is often demonstrated when it comes to solving mysteries and catching criminals while the adults "bumble around helplessly" (WATSON 204). Children are "portrayed as more observant, more energetic, and having a greater capacity for believing the unusual than the adult" (ibid.). They are more effective than adults, which becomes most obvious in KÄSTNER's *Emil und die Detektive* (1930), generally considered one of the forerunners of current detective fiction, and BLYTON's *Famous Five* (1942) and *Secret Seven* (1949).

Child heroes in realistic mystery and detective fiction

Preferred settings for mystery and crime fiction are secret passages, haunted houses, buried treasures, and all kinds of disguise, which point at the close connection of the genre to adventure stories in children's fiction. In teenage detective fiction, teenagers often act in groups and gangs. However, some current novels such as HOROWITZ's *Stormbreaker* also center around single heroes, modeled on the James Bond hero figure.

Settings

In popular crime fiction teenagers solve puzzles both in fast-paced, often formulaic and serialized stories and in more challenging creative texts.

Chapter 2   Young adult fiction for EFL learners

Popular series and challenging crime stories

Nancy Drew, *The Hardy Boys* or *Alfred Hitchcock and The Three Investigators* series provide light entertainment. More challenging titles of higher literary quality, in which it is not so easy to differentiate between the "bad and the good guy" include Forest's *The Thuggery Affair* (1965) and Bawden's *The Witch's Daughter* (1966). In both novels, the protagonists' and the criminals' ambiguity is exposed.

Combination of problem novel and mystery

In current teenage fiction, the mystery genre often contains elements of the problem novel. For example, *Abomination* and *Holes* can be read both as mystery and crime stories and as problem stories. Reading *Abomination* as a crime novel puts the question of who "Abomination" is, of who imprisoned him and of how the boy can be released and reunited with his mother into the foreground.

Reading a problem novel as a mystery

In *Holes*, the puzzle of whether the boys find the treasure, whose property it is, how the boys' innocence can be proved, and whether or not the criminal camp guards will be arrested has to be solved (see also chapter 3). Reading the novels as mysteries means that they have to be read faster. To best train fast reading, the reading process should not be interrupted by too many exercises and discussion questions. With mysteries, students should be able to learn to read quickly because they want to know "who done it".

Recommendations for the secondary classroom
Grade 5–6

Wendelin van Draanen:
Shredderman 1 Secret Identity

> For lower intermediate learners, Van Draanen's *Shredderman series* should be appropriate if some annotations are made, especially for the colloquial style. Brian Biggs' hilarious illustrations of *Shredderman* in black-and-white cartoon form are very popular among native speakers and should be for learners of English, too.
> *Secret Identity* is about a brainy fifth grader named Nolan Byrd, who is called "nerd" by the school bully Bubba Bixby who cheats, lies, steals, and terrorizes classmates. Tired of Bubba's tormenting, Nolan secretly and anonymously launches the website "shredderman. com" as a class project, an online forum that chronicles the bully's actions.

Marjorie Weinman Sharmat & Marc Simont: *Nate the Great Goes Down in the Dumps*

> For young readers, the *Nate the Great* books are a good starting point. They might appear a bit childish, but are easy to read, short, and are accompanied by funny pictures.

7   Mystery: crime and detective novels

Grade 7–8

The Secret Seven (1949) and *Famous Five* (1942) series by ENID BLYTON, are still popular and are a good starting point for extensive reading at a relatively early age. The fact that learners have probably read some of the books in German some time ago might help them to enjoy reading in English when they recognize some of the stories. The print material, also available in simplified form, is accompanied by computer games, comics, video TV series, and DVDs.

ENID BLYTON: *The Secret Seven* and *Famous Five* series

Grade 9–10

When Salim gets on board the London Eye, his cousins see him wave to them. But after half an hour, Salim does not get off the famous Ferris Wheel on the banks of the River Thames. He seems to have vanished from the earth. Since the police are worthless, Ted, the autistic narrator, and his older sister Kat become detectives. The two teenagers overcome their differences to follow a trail of clues across London. And it is Ted with his strange ideas who finds the answer to the mystery.

SIOBHAN DOWD: *London Eye Mystery*

SIOBHAN DOWD also wrote *A Swift Pure Cry*, a novel about a poor Irish girl who becomes pregnant, unwillingly and unknowingly. This exciting story, although it is more of a problem novel, can be read as a mystery too.

SWINDELLS' *Stone Cold*, winner of the English Carnegie Medal in 1993, is not called a "mystery" novel, but it is definitely very suspenseful. Link, the main character runs away from a violent bullying stepfather to the streets of London. He is stalked by a bitter ex-sergeant and sex offender who calls himself 'Shelter'. Link gets caught, as many other homeless youngsters do, but meanwhile he has befriended and Gail, who helps him to get free. In 1997, the novel was adapted into a film with the same title, but it is rarely available any more. Standerline's 72-page drama version accompanied by some drama activities was published in 1999.

ROBERT SWINDELLS: *Stone Cold*

Both SMITH's *Zach's Lie* (2001) and the sequel *Zach's Run* (2005) are suspenseful. The protagonist has to hide under a new identity since drug smugglers are out to take revenge on Zach and his father for a crime that he committed (unwillingly). The father was imprisoned but has agreed to cooperate with the police to be released prematurely.

ROLAND SMITH: *Zach's Lie*

Chapter 2 Young adult fiction for EFL learners

Reluctant readers

Brian Vaughan: *Runaways*

> The graphic series *Runaways*, told by Brian Vaughan, is a very unusual work in which six rich Hollywood parents turn out to be criminals. The characters of their six teenage sons and daughters are well-rounded with relatively few words but with good graphic design. Every year they all meet as a group, separate from their parents' secret convention. One year they finally realize that the adults are criminals belonging to a secret society. When the police do not intervene, the teenagers form a group of detectives to find out what their parents' scheme is. Since it is suspenseful and not as difficult to decipher as some other graphic novels, it is definitely a series that should be in class libraries or book cases from grade 9 on.

Girls' books – boys' books

All recommended books are probably highly suspenseful for both sexes since in most cases boys and girls cooperate to arrest criminals or solve criminal cases. Maybe some more of the formulaic, extremely popular Enid Blyton stories and films could be part of a class library.

Other suspenseful works will be the focus in the chapter 2.9 dealing with horror and ghost stories.

> **TIP**
> Read a formulaic detective story of one of the popular series and a more challenging crime story such as the short, highly recommended novella An Eye for an Eye by black English writer Malorie Blackman. Make a list of the elements of crime fiction she uses. Connected are elements of the problem novel. Discuss what age group you would use it for in class.

8 Fantasy

Definition

Fantasy tells of the presence of magic or the supernatural in an otherwise realistic, familiar world. The fantastic world is manifested in the form of magical beings, objects, or events, anchored in reality.

Sub-genres

There are many subgenres of fantasy: fairy tales, myths, legends, science fiction, utopias, and dystopias. The difference between the subgenres fairy tales, folk tales, legends and myth on the one hand and fantasy on the other hand is that the former were originally transmitted orally whereas fantasy is created by specific authors. Another difference is that fairy tales are wholly set in a magic world and its heroes do not question the magic of this fantasy realm. Here I will not focus on fairy tales, myths, and legends, although all fantasy literature constantly draws upon fairy tale and mythological elements.

T0DOROV, in his theory of the fantastic in literature, differentiates between "the marvelous", "the fantastic", and "the uncanny" (TODOROV 1972). "The marvelous" comprises fairy tales and other wonder tales, and in "the fantastic" and "the uncanny" the protagonist is confronted with the supernatural. What all fantasy stories have in common is a basic plot similar to the plot of the adventure story: The hero leaves home, the familiar place, meets helpers and opponents, goes through trials in a strange world, and returns home after gaining some form of spiritual or financial wealth (cf. NIKOLAJEVA in ZIPES 2: 58ff.). They are about heroes' quests, often about a combat between good and evil forces in all kinds of forms.

TODOROV on fantasy

Fantasy may be set in wholly fantastic worlds that are entire universes in themselves; it may set out in the real world and move on to other worlds, or it may switch between the real and the fantastic worlds. Often stories start out in what TOLKIEN in "On Fairy Stories" calls the "Primary" world, the real world and end in the "Secondary" world, the fantastic, imagined, magical world. According to TOLKIEN, characters all share extraordinary powers or sensibilities, which are enhanced by certain "tools" and companions, either humans or animals or other magical companions. Writers' imaginations allow them to transform and modernize original fairy tale elements such as magic wands, swords and lanterns, flying carpets and horses, witches and goblins, and magic food and drink, but their functions remain basically the same. In contrast to fairy tales, myths, and legends, characters in fantasy are ordinary people; they may be scared and reluctant to perform a task, or they may even fail (cf. NIKOLAJEVA in ZIPES 2: 61). Fantasy writers often assure their readers: "they are just like you".

TOLKIEN on fantasy

The relationship between text and reader is a special one: it is based on the belief that the world and the events depicted are true. Protagonist and reader share the dilemma of experiencing two different worlds; the reader accepts magic as part of the world created by the author. Magic adventures and visions can be rationally accepted as protagonists' dreams, hallucinations, fever (*King of Shadows*), or mental or emotional disturbance (cf. NIKOLAJEVA in ZIPES 2: 60).

Relationship between text and reader

In most novels the two worlds are not totally separate. For example, in PULLMAN's *His Dark Materials* it is the real world of Oxford University from which the girl protagonist Lyra travels. In ROWLING's *Harry Potter and the Philosopher's Stone* the real world that the neglected and abused 11-year-old orphan Harry escapes from is the "Muggles' world". At Hogwarts he finds his home. Harry, who was accident-prone and always

Relationship between the two worlds

involved in mysterious situations in the real world, realizes that he is unique, but neither a monster nor a superhero. He has to learn the hard way and he needs his ultimate strength to withstand Valdemort. "Hogwart provides for Harry and the reader an alternative, contemporaneous, thoroughly developed society in which one can creatively, realistically, and usefully stretch one's mind within new limits of suffering and hope" (TOTARO: 133). Like Harry Potter, Jonas, the 12-year-old protagonist of *The Giver*, is suffering from isolation in his socially engineered "brave new" world, especially when he realizes he can "see beyond". Saving a child, he flees to "elsewhere", another world: and that's where he hopes his real home will be.

The special appeal of *Twilight*

One example of a strange encounter of the two worlds which is currently extraordinarily popular, is MEYER's *Twilight*. Set in the very ordinary world in Forks on the Olympic Peninsula, the rainiest spot in the USA close to the Pacific Ocean in Washington State, the supernatural appears in the shape of Edward, the vampire. Seventeen-year-old sophomore Bella has decided to live with her father in Forks, goes to high school, and has the usual – in this case positive – experiences of a newcomer at a small town high school. She is not attracted to a variety of real high school admirers, but to the vampire Edward, another sophomore at the same school who looks like a haughty Greek god. Edward tells her he was born more than 100 years ago and was adopted by the town's doctor, another vampire born almost 400 years ago. Both high school students get entangled in a very complicated affair, with sensitive, considerate Edward always afraid of the lethal danger that his vampire impulses may pose for her. In the first part of the trilogy he uses his powers to save Bella from another, very dangerous vampire attacker, and after her recovery at a hospital, the reader finds them together at a high school prom.

The reason for the outstanding popularity of this (long) trilogy about the relationship between a very ordinary girl and a vampire seems to be that the fantastic is a metaphor for reality, as NIKOLAJEVA suggests (cf. ZIPES 2: 62). Edward and Bella are fascinated by each other, but the idea of the strangeness of any partner in a love relationship is well depicted: the attraction, the fear of coming too close, the danger of destruction and of being destroyed by the other. Edward is highly sensitive to the danger that he poses for Bella and he tries to save her, but cannot stay away from her. There is a physical, chemical attraction (her scent!) that he cannot evade. Another reason for the trilogy's popularity is definitely the easy, everyday language. A Harry Potter-like craze, mostly among girls, makes it possible for them to read the 500+ page novels in English!

In 2008, a number of similar novels appeared that deal with encounters with the dead, so-called "zombie novels" including *Zombie Blondes* and *Generation Dead*. Both novels adhere to the conventions of horror films, taking place in sleepy-seeming "Anytowns" where the heroines fall in

love with handsome dead guys. They fight, too, but what they are really fighting is oppression and rejection in small town communities and high schools (cf. MARLER: 14).
Within the imaginative fantasy genre there is a general distinction between animal and toy stories, a subgenre popular in the 19th century (*The Nutcracker*), in which animals and toys can talk (*Watership Down; The Indian in the Cupboard*), extraordinary characters and extraordinary worlds (*James and the Giant Peach, Skellig, Artemis Fowl, Ender's Game*), magical powers and suspense and the supernatural (*Harry Potter, Ella Enchanted, The Stormbreaker*), time shift and imaginary realms (*King of Shadows, Sang Spell*), high fantasy (*The Hobbit, His Dark Materials, The Chronicles of Prydain*), and all kinds of science fiction, in which technology reigns.

Children's literature experts argue that fantasy has a greater power to invent alternative worlds than other kinds of fiction. They see its chief contribution to readers of all ages in the visionary aspect of fantasy, "its power to tweak and nurture the imagination", (cf. CONTINUUM ENCYCLOPEDIA ONLINE). NIKOLAJEVA attributes its attraction to the human realization of discontent with the existing reality and a hope for a better future. She argues that in troubled times when advanced technological societies "have gone awry" and a strong impulse for social change is visible, people need utopian and dystopian literature more than ever (cf. HINTZ & OSTRY Ix). NIKOLAJEVA contends that "fantasy allows writers to deal with psychological, ethical, and existential questions in a slightly detached manner, which frequently proves more effective with young readers than straightforward realism" (ZIPES 2: 62).

Alternative worlds

Many fantasy novels are far too long to be read in the EFL classrooms. They may be read individually by students who have a book report/review assignment, but teachers dealing with 500–1000 page books in the EFL classrooms is hard to imagine (cf. VOLKMANN 2000). If the majority of a class likes fantasy, TOLKIEN's *The Hobbit* (1937) accompanied by its graphic form and the movie would be plausible. Also, excerpts of the Harry Potter series have proved to work (cf. RÖLLICH-FABER 2003, KÜPPERS 2001). The following novels of rather modest volume seem appropriate for EFL readers.

Recommendations for the secondary classroom
Grade 6–7

For more advanced 6th to 7th graders, Louis Sachar's funny and almost "off the wall" *Wayside School* series seems appropriate since it consists of stories that can be read separately. Comprehension of the humorous stories will be easier if they are first read aloud by the teacher or a native speaker.
Like DAHL, SACHAR draws on children's experiences of their power-

LOUIS SACHAR: *Sideways Stories from Wayside School*

Chapter 2 Young adult fiction for EFL learners

lessness at school to tell humorous stories of role reversal. The first story, tells about a teacher who turns children into apples and later turns herself into one, which the yard teacher ends up eating (unknowingly). However, the children are not gleefully happy since they did not wish such a bad end on their idiosyncratic teacher.

Grade 7–8

SID FLEISCHMAN & PETER SIS: *The Whipping Boy*

The Whipping Boy is a "prince and the pauper" story, in which through purposeful role reversal the prince and the pauper learn lessons for life. Prince Horace (called "Prince Brat") is the nasty prince, but Jemmy, the street boy, gets the whippings for Brat's nastiness. The two boys escape, because Prince Brat decides he is bored with his royal life and needs some adventure. Although Jemmy has devised plans for his own escape, the prince forces Jemmy to join him to carry his picnic basket. On the run and having been captured by two highwaymen and murderers, Jemmy has to write a ransom note to the king, because Brat, who is always occupied with pranks, never learned to read and write. The two highwaymen and murderers take Jemmy to be the prince, because Jemmy is brave, strong, smart, and literate. Soon, however, the outlaws realize that Jemmy is a former street child and the whipping boy and that Prince Horace is the true prince. When the prince hears a lady call him "Prince Brat" (which nobody ever did to his face, only behind his back), he is horrified by the name and improves his behavior. Full of regret and repentance, he goes back to the castle and asks his father, the King, to pardon Jemmy. His father gives Jemmy royal protection, provided the prince does his lessons.

The story is relatively short, draws on a fairy-tale formula, is very funny, and should thus be an enrichment for younger readers. The author and illustrator received the Newbery Medal for the book in 1986.

Other fantasy books for younger readers are abundant. Small novels in the *Space Brat* series by BRUCE & CATHERINE COLVILLE are short, funny, and contain illustrations as does the magic realm fantasy series *The Dragon of Doom* by the same authors.

DAVID ALMOND: *Skellig*

Twelve-year-old Michael, who likes to play soccer, tells the story of the discovery of and encounter with Skellig, the mysterious, angel-like creature living in an old shed on the rundown property his parents have just bought. Shortly thereafter, he meets Mina, a home-schooled girl with a passion for William Blake's poetry and a great interest in birds. The two take Skellig to an empty house where they want to nurse him back to health and also offer him companionship. Skellig disappears as suddenly as he appeared. The mystery of the creature, where he comes from and where he went, whether he was an angel or a "hobo" is never resolved. But the two children learn something about the subtle line between life and death, not only through Skellig, but also through the experience of Michael's baby sister's almost deadly disease.

Grade 9–10

The Giver is one of the most popular fantasy novels for children and teenagers of the last two decades. In the USA, it is a standard novel for 5th–7th graders, but I believe it is best suited for 9th–11th graders in Germany. Among other issues, it is about the moral decision a 12-year-old must make in order to save the life of a baby who is scheduled to be killed because it does not fit into the community of streamlined humans. In this community, illness, war, and fear do not exist; however, the absence of these negative qualities of life also corresponds with the absence of sex, love, colors, and even of weather. The ruling principle in the "brave new world" of *The Giver* is sameness. Everybody is to be the same. Every day is the same. There are no highlights, no lowlights. Children are not born of natural parents; children, one of each sex, are assigned to each family unit by the authorities, the Committee of Elders. There is no freedom of choice and even jobs are assigned. In this world, Jonas, the selected "Receiver of Memories", is the only one to whom the painful and beautiful memories of the past are transmitted; the rest of the community lives without any memory of the past.

The Giver is best suited for grades 9–10, because at that age many youths ask themselves questions about the society they live in and the freedom they enjoy or lack. Readers should be older than 12 to be able to fully understand the dangerous implications of the seemingly perfect society. The age of the protagonist only reflects the archaic initiation age of a young person into the adult world. It seems to me that American children read it before they have reached the maturity level necessary to fully understand the concept. For the author Lois Lowry, *The Giver*, like all of her 35 books, gives children hope that they are able to make moral choices (cf. http://www.loislowry.com; HINTZ & OSTRY 1996).

LOIS LOWRY: The Giver

Among the Hidden is set in the near future of shortages and deprivation, where widespread famines have led to a totalitarian government that controls all aspects of its citizens' lives. Born as a third child ("shadow child") at a time when having more than two children per family is illegal, Luke has spent all of his 12 years in hiding. At first he is allowed to go outside, since his family's farmhouse is miles away from anything else, but when the woods are cut and new houses are

MARGARET HADDIX PETERSON: Among the Hidden

built, he is no longer permitted outside and has to stay hidden in the attic all the time.

One day, when he is bored again and gazes across at the house of their new neighbors, he spies a child's face at a window after the neighbors' family of four has already left for the day. Then it occurs to him that he might not be the only hidden child. He ventures across the yard to enter the neighbors' house and meets Jen, another shadow child. Jen is much more outgoing and brave than Luke and has already contacted other illegal children via internet chat rooms. She even organizes a rally to demonstrate against their illegal status and summons all her contacts, including Luke, to participate. Since Luke is too shy and cowardly, but finally proves to have a better sense of reality, she goes out alone to lead the demonstration. All 40 participants are shot. How Luke finds out about this is a very exciting story involving the Government's Population Police. The idea of a totalitarian system limiting the free will and the private decisions of its citizens provides lots of issues for class discussion. Students who have enjoyed *Among the Hidden* will probably continue reading its sequels.

PHILLIS RAYNOLDS NAYLOR:
Sang Spell

Sang Spell reads more like a haunting mystery than a fantasy story. What makes it a fantasy novel is the strange place where Josh wakes up after being mugged and left beside a remote mountain road on a hitchhiking trip to Dallas. A woman driving a horse and cart takes him to a mysterious, Amish-like village, with no cars, telephones, or electricity. The villagers turn out to be the Melungeons, a long-lost people of mixed ethnicity. Josh's questions concerning the village are never answered directly so he neither knows where he is nor how to get out. He befriends a young woman his own age while they gather ginseng ("sang"), but she does not tell him either. He frequently tries to escape, but has little success, since all roads he takes lead back to this village. Only when Josh joins in the villagers' rituals and celebrations, and his loyalty to the Melungeons is tested, does he find himself free to leave.

SUSAN COOPER:
King of Shadows

Only in the world of theater can Nat Field find an escape from the tragedies that have overshadowed his young life. Therefore, he is very excited when he is chosen to join an American drama company travelling to London to perform "A Midsummer Night's Dream" in the new Globe Theatre. When he gets sick in England, Nat wakes up and is transported four hundred years back in time to a Shakespearean production of "A Midsummer Night's Dream". In Shakespeare he finds the warm, nurturing father figure that he lacks in real life.

8 Fantasy

The book is a traditional time travel story that can also be used well in connection with the study of Shakespeare's plays. Cooper describes the setting so vividly that it makes the Elizabethan age come to life.

Reluctant readers

FIONA FRENCH: *Snow White in New York*

This short graphic novel is an imitation of the classic GRIMMS' fairy tale *Snow White and the Seven Dwarves*. The classic characters are transferred into a rich New York society of the 1920s, where Snow White's stepmother orders her bodyguards to kill her. Jazz musicians are the ones who take her in to perform with them and thus she becomes more famous than her stepmother, the classiest dame in New York. The stepmother invites Snow White to a party and poisons her. Finally, when her coffin is carried by the jazz musicians, the poisoned cherry falls from her mouth.

Readers will not only be delighted with this easy-to-understand fairy tale, but they will also get an introduction to New York life through the pictures. The clear, almost cubist drawings and colorful paintings are reminiscent of the "roaring twenties", but the story could have happened any time today. The story is recommended for weaker readers in grades 7–9.

ANTHONY BROWNE'S *King Kong*

For older readers, the re-creation of *King Kong* by ANTHONY BROWNE is mentioned here. Although the text is rather long and complex, readers can draw on their knowledge of the original *King Kong* story by Wallace and Cooper, which was made into a highly popular film. If the novel is read by the whole class, especially the art work of the graphic novel and the film should be compared.

More text recommendations for reluctant readers, can be found in chapter 2,10.

Girls' books – boys' books

All of the recommended fantasy novels can be read and enjoyed by both males and females. In predominantly male classes, the graphic novel and film *Stormbreaker*, about a boy spy and superhero who is equipped with unnatural forces and extraordinary devices, should be considered (see chapter 2,10). Also science fiction novels set in space or the ones with a lot of technological detail seem to be read by boys, whereas girls prefer "soft science fiction".

> **TIP** *The appeal of fantasy books is greater than ever. Interview teenagers and find out why* Ender's Game, Harry Potter, His Dark Materials, Twilight *and other fantasy books are so popular.*

Chapter 2 Young adult fiction for EFL learners

9 Ghost and horror stories

Definition

Ghost and horror stories are stories of the supernatural that play upon the desire of many children and adults to be pleasurably frightened and terrified. In Shakespeare's *The Winter's Tale*, Queen Hermione begs her little son 'to do your best/To fright me with your sprites'. He 'will do it softly' and begins at once: 'There was a man dwelt by a churchyard ...' (cf. THE CAMBRIDGE GUIDE TO CHILDREN'S BOOKS ONLINE). Like in many EDGAR ALLAN POE stories, characters often cross the boundaries between the living and the dead and one sometimes does not know whether ghosts are more real than humans. Such stories blend elements of Gothic horror with cryptic settings filled with castles, tombs, labyrinth paths, and dark gloomy rooms" (cf. PARINI 4: 11).

The popularity of ghost and horror stories

At the start of the new millennium, horror and ghost stories are widely popular among children, teenagers, and adults with new vampire, zombie, and ghost stories appearing for all ages. MEYER's *Twilight* Trilogy is an example of another crossover novel that is read by teenagers and adults alike. I have encountered students of the *Realschule* who read these books in the original in spite of their volume. The same was true for the *Harry Potter* books before they were published in German. Motivation sometimes works wonders!

One appeal of horror stories is that the dark, strange side of human nature is encountered in a seemingly familiar realm. This is the case in classic EDGAR ALLAN POE stories, and it is true for *Twilight* and the rather dark, challenging YA novel *Coraline*.

Recommendations for the secondary classroom
Grade 5–6

ELIZABETH LEVY:
Frankenstein Moved in on the Fourth Floor* and *Dracula Is a Pain in the Neck

Frankenstein Moved in on the Fourth Floor is about a mysterious man's noises that the young protagonist hears in his multistory house. He tries to find out what "Frankenstein" is up to.
LEVY's *Dracula Is a Pain in the Neck* is also about mysteriously haunting noises which can be heard at a camp. Both stories are rather humorous.

Grade 7–8

KATE CULHANE & MICHAEL HAGUE:
A Ghost Story

The tale in this picture book is based on a traditional Irish story "The Blood Drawing Ghost", which was later published by Jeremiah Curtin in the collection *Tales of the Faeries and of the Ghost World*. It is a typical ghost story in which a dead person comes back to life and haunts a poor woman who is mourning her mother in a graveyard. She has to carry him into the house of a rich merchant. There he draws blood from the three sleeping sons and forces the woman to cook it and eat it with porridge. The three sons who die after this scene come back to life through the heroic deed of the young woman, who is later allowed to marry the oldest son. This book should be read aloud in a dark room!

Grade 9–10

After Coraline and her busy parents have moved into an old house located on a huge lot with strange tenants and pets living above and below them, she finds a wooden door at the far corner of the living room. Of course, she is extremely curious. She unlocks it but on her first attempt it opens only onto a brick wall. However, when she opens it again later, she finds a dark hallway in front of her. On the other side she finds even more: everything nearly mirrors their real apartment (including the wallpaper), but not all is exactly the same. There is something eerie about it that fascinates her. And then she finds her parents there too, but they do not have real eyes; in the place of eyes they have buttons, they have extraordinarily white skin, and they seem more possessive than normal. What she experiences is a twisted version of the familiar world, and that is what makes it scary. Moreover, these "other" parents do not want to let her leave.

The novel's beginning is reminiscent of *The Lion, the Witch, and the Wardrobe* and *Alice in Wonderland* with its opening door/hole to another world but it is far scarier. The black illustrations by British artist DAVE MCKEAN *(The Sandmann)* emphasize the story's quiet horror. This book is also available as a graphic novel.

NEIL GAIMAN:
Coraline

Reluctant readers

When Lucy takes the noises in the walls of her house seriously and wants to warn her family, they want to explain them away rationally and thus say they are only caused by mice, rats, or bats. All of them say: "If the wolves come out from the walls it's all over". Lucy fails to understand and remains puzzled. When the wolves really do come out, the family flees from the house and each member thinks of a different place to escape to. Lucy, however, slips back into the house to get her pig-puppet and discovers that there is space in the walls to live in. Finally the whole family joins her in the walls of the house. From there they observe the wolves doing strange things. The family decides to reclaim the house and the wolves flee.

In contrast to many other "children's writers", British author GAIMAN tackles themes that are frightening for children and disturbing for

NEIL GAIMAN &
DAVE MCKEAN:
The Wolves in the Walls

adults. In much of his fiction children see things that adults do not (want to) see and it is the children who confront the threats (cf. Grilli in ZIPES 2: 114).

Although the story is fairy-tale-like, the artwork of Dave McKean is very challenging. Teenagers could analyze some of the art, its paintings and drawings, frames, borders, colors, letters, and create their own story.

MICHAEL MUCCI
& BILL HALIAR:
Dracula
(Graphic novel)

Dracula stands for horror stories. This edition is an abbreviated and simplified graphic novel version of BRAM STOKER's *Dracula*. The images pay close attention to detail, from facial expressions to costuming and setting. Thus they convey the original novel's text, tone, mood, and atmosphere very well.

R.L. STINE:
The Goosebumps series

The Goosebumps series appears rather "cheap". Yet the *Goosebumps* and the *HorrorLand* series are extremely popular worldwide. Each story ends with a cliffhanger and is continued in subsequent books and on the internet. The first title of the series is "Revenge of the Living Dummy." The fast-paced series is good for class libraries, since they will probably encourage even reluctant readers to read. Films of the *Goosebumps* series will possibly improve reading comprehension and motivation.

Girls' books – boys' books

In ghost and horror stories gender does not play a role. If girls like horror stories, they will most likely read the same stories boys read.

> **TIP** Reread or listen to Poe's "The Tell-Tale Heart". In this short story you will find all elements of a scary story. List the elements. Then watch the short film (available from Landesbildstellen) and see which element this medium adds.

10 Superheroes

Superhero definition

Many stories of superhero adventures are based on the original cartoon art of the 1920s to the 1960s. Superhero characters usually have dual identities combining human and divine aspects. Modest alter egos protect superhero operations either in disguise or simply as the transformed self (schoolboy Billy Batson changes into fully-grown *Captain Marvel*, scientist Bruce Banner changes into the *Incredible Hulk*, 1962). Alter egos, possibly unattractive and looked down upon, often contrast radically with superhero. "Dualism occurs in many forms: blending human and animal nature (a man with the power of a bat or spider), or mirroring and merging with the evil nature of the foe to understand it" (CAMBRIDGE GUIDE TO CHILDREN'S BOOKS ONLINE).

In his introduction to SMITH's contemporary remaking of the classic comic *Shazam* Alex Ross explains the popularity of superhero comics by relating it to the idea of "charm", which superheroes embody like no other. "The titans of myth found a new home in our rainbow clad friends, and the world needs their creative stimulus" (SMITH 2007: 5). Smith himself writes in his afterword that he found his inspiration in myths and fairy tales such as *Arabian Nights* (209).

Contemporary superheroes

Many teenagers know about superheroes from popular films, many of which reappeared almost simultaneously in 2008 (e.g. *Iron Man, The Dark Knight, The Incredible Hulk, The Spirit*). Not every teenager knows the ancient folktales, fairy tales, and myths they are based on (cf. RICH 2008). Reading these stories in class might be a chance to relate these superhero tales to Greek myths and fairy tales, which might shed new light on the old tales.

Ancient myths and beliefs as a base for superhero adventures

Neither does every fan see the references to Christian beliefs that PLOTINSKY points out (http: www.city-journal.org). In the first *Superman* film (1978), a clear reference to "God" the father sending his son to earth is visible. In later installments, Superman says: "You wrote that the world does not need a savior, but every day I hear people crying for one." Superman's outstretched hands at right angles to his body and legs is reminiscent of the crucified figure. Obviously there are "inherent messianic qualities in the concept of the superhero - an individual with exceptional qualities who sacrifices part of his or her life for the greater good" (MCKEE in http:www.city-journal.org).

Nowadays, superheroes and -heroines are given special attention even in "high art" institutions. In 2008, the Metropolitan Museum of Art in New York dedicated an exhibition to their costumes, and in 2009 the Jewish Museum in Frankfurt showed many Jewish-American cartoon artists' work. It was stunning to see that in the first few decades of the 20th century, Jewish-Americans – in their wish for assimilation into American society – created "all-American" characters who were everything but outsiders (see also chapter 2.2).

Superheroes in "high art" institutions

Another sign of the growing acceptance of the genre in high art is the re-creation of superheroes and -heroines by renowned adult writers: For example, in 2007, JODI PICOULT rewrote the original *Wonder Woman* story, published by William Moulton Marston in 1941, as *Wonder Woman. Love and Murder*. This recreation is clearly for an adult audience.

Chapter 2   Young adult fiction for EFL learners

Superheroes for young learners

New simplified series about superheroes from various educational publishers seem especially appropriate for reluctant readers and slower learners. They are both good for and popular among teenagers whose EFL reading skills are still rudimentary, since their protagonists are not children. Graded readers usually have four levels of difficulty, from level 1: "Learning and beginning to read" up through level 4: "Proficient readers".

For younger audiences, graded readers from level 1: *Batman and Spiderman* to level 4: *Greatest Battles* and *Star Wars Galactic Crisis* are a good introduction to the lives of these strong, muscular superheroes who fight evil in the world with specific machinery and weapons. All these superheroes like Spiderman, Hulk, the Fantastic Four, Galactus, Wolverine, to name only a few, have magic powers which help them defeat wicked supervillains. Superheroines like Jane Grey, Wonder Woman, and Spiderwoman were created as well, but to my knowledge have not yet been turned into educational material so far.

Recommendations for the secondary classroom
Grade 5–8

SAUNDERS, CATHERINE: *Spiderman. The Amazing Story* (level 1)

> Highly recommendable for grades 5 and 6 and older "reluctant readers" are the *Batman* and *Spiderman* series. They are graded readers with full-color illustrations based on the original Batman and Spiderman art. The simple illustrations and easy-to-follow text will make this an enjoyable reading experience while creating a level of suspense and excitement.

SCOTT CIENCIN & RICK BURCHETT: *Batman* (level 3)

> The Scholastic reader series *Batman* should be appropriate from grade 6 on. In several small volumes it tells the story of how Batman fights evil in New York ("Gotham City").

CATHERINE SAUNDERS: *Star Wars. The Story of Darth Vader* (level 3)

> *Star Wars. The Story of Darth Vader* is more complex and should be appropriate from grade 7 on. Teens will know the story from TV and should therefore be able to comprehend the content much better. For experts, it should serve as an appropriate basis for a presentation in class.

MICHAEL RYAN: *Teenage Mutant Ninja Turtles*

> Another superhero series is the "Cine-Manga" series. The original Eastman & Lair comic book from 1984 was turned into the *Teenage Mutant Ninja Turtles* TV series (1987–1996; 2003-present) and a feature film.
> When the New York police is unable to stop a severe crime wave, the four turtle vigilantes named after famous Italian painters, under the

leadership of Splinter, fight to save the city. The clear, black and white speech squares in the Tokyopop edition help make the story a quick read.

Grade 9–10

The level 4 readers such as *Marvel Heroes Greatest Battles*, *Star Wars Galactic Crisis!* and *The Incredible Hulk* of the DK graded reader series are not easy for beginning learners, but are very good for teenagers who will be motivated by the illustrations, which are partly based on original cartoons (*Batman*, *Hulk*) and films (*Star Wars*). I assume teenage fans will skip over unknown vocabulary since they already have a good deal of knowledge about their favorite heroes. *The Incredible Hulk* is informative as well, informing its young audience about the history of the Cold War and nuclear testing, a time in which many of the comics were created.

MATTHEW MANNING:
Marvel Heroes Greatest Battles

RYDER WINDHAM:
Star Wars Galactic Crisis!

MICHAEL TEITELBAUM:
The Incredible Hulk

In *Shazam*, Captain Marvel, the 1940's superhero, is reintroduced for a young adult audience. Billy Batson, a young homeless orphan living in the streets of New York, follows a mysterious figure into the subway and is taken to a wizard. The wizard is a wise man who tells him the secrets of the world. From then on Billy is transformed into Captain Marvel when he speaks the word "Shazam". But the wizard also warns Billy not to ever go to a secret place on top of a mountain, which is reserved for eternity. Of course, Billy does not listen, which causes evil powers to endanger him and the world at large. Thus the greatest danger, a seemingly political robot monster, causes danger for the whole city. The story is obviously modeled after post-9/11 New York.

This comic is well suited for older intermediate readers (from grade 9 on). It could be used in the classroom and for individual reading. There will be comic fans who have some previous knowledge of the original Captain Marvel comic books. These fans will be amazed, or maybe disappointed, by the radical changes Jeff Smith made. Newcomers, however, will be entertained by Smith's lively reinvention.

JEFF SMITH:
Shazam

Currently, Japanese manga are very popular among young adult readers. The Japanese cartoon book, based on the film *Howl's Moving Castle*, which is itself based on the fantasy novel by DIANNA WYNNE-JONES, should be another motivating read for reluctant readers who need visual literacy to understand the comic book. Apart from the beginning, however, the book and film are quite different.

HAYAO MIYAZAKI:
Howl's Moving Castle
(volume 1–4)

Chapter 2   Young adult fiction for EFL learners

Girls' books – boys' books

ANTHONY HOROWITZ: *Stormbreaker*

HOROWITZ's graphic novel *Stormbreaker* could be another option for predominantly male classes. From my female perspective, I cannot imagine many girls being interested in this action-packed, gadget-crazy, superhero spy novel. However, many males obviously enjoy this kind of teenage hero story and even need it to deal with the power imbalance of teenagers and to develop into mature adults (cf. NEWKIRK 117f.).

The graphic novel was modeled on HOROWITZ's long novel with the same title, which itself was made into a movie. It was drawn by KANAKO and YUZURU, two Japanese women whose style is clear, less confusing than some other superhero mangas, and more varied. The colors, hues, and shades are selected carefully to match the setting and the fast-paced action. Hero Alex Rider moves between many places – from his elegant London house to the rough military training camp in Wales to the secret lab and home of the villain Mr. Sayle – from where he sets out to save the world. Evil Mr Sayle is intent on destroying the British school children, pretending to give each of them computers infiltrated with a deadly virus. For him, this is revenge for being bullied as an immigrant at his posh English boarding school that the Prime Minister attended too!

Boys who want to read the whole story, should read the novel *Stormbreaker*, which is part of HOROWITZ's *Alex Rider* series. Any of HOROWITZ's numerous modern adventure, superhero books are extremely popular among boys internationally.

If girls are interested in female superheroes at all, they might relate to *Spider Woman, Wonder Woman*, or other books in the genre with heroines at the center. Superheroines like Jean Grey fight alongside fellow X-Men, and Wonder Woman is a founding member of a league fighting for justice.

For all popular comic and graphic novels, a certain amount of knowledge of current teen language is necessary. Teachers or student experts should make a list of the teen vernacular to assist the readers. Very commonly-used words are "awesome, dropout, freak (out), trash etc., words that teenagers want to know, since they are not part of what they call "school English".

> **TIP**
>
> *Many teachers have never read any comics, since in Germany, as well as in the USA, they were initially considered bad literature. Read as much as you can and see to what extent comics differ in style and content.*
>
> *In a group of students/teachers, design a 4-hour teaching unit based on your (real and imagined) classroom using one of the superhero texts. Give one of the comics to a reluctant reader, who is a comics expert, and have him/her present the book in class.*
>
> *In 2006, the PBS (Public Broadcasting Service) educational TV series "Wordgirl" was created. It is an animated program featuring superheroine Becky Botsford, alias Wordgirl, who defeats dangerous villains by using specific words. This program can help middle school learners to expand their vocabulary. The series may have appeared on DVD by now. Check it out! (pbskidsgo.org/wordgirl)*

11 Short stories

Since learners have been exposed to short stories in textbooks, I will not dwell long on this particular genre. Through short stories students have become used to reading texts which seldom exceed the 1–2-page textbook format.

Short stories' condensed form

Most short stories in anthologies for children and young adults are longer. The short story, a forerunner of the novel, usually follows the same pattern but is more to the point, more condensed. It intensifies the narrative process. It can be compared to a photography, drawing the reader's attention to a moment which simultaneously notices the frame and looks beyond it (cf. ISAAC in ZIPES 3: 453).

Short stories written for teenagers have a great potential for student response. There are a significant number of anthologies of theme-based or author-based short stories.

Recommendations for the secondary classroom
Grade 5–8

Short stories for younger learners are to be found in collections written for them in shortened, simplified, and illustrated versions. There are also Dracula, vampire, and zombie stories, such as HOROWITZ's *Horror Stories*. Horror stories have been published for all learners' levels by various educational publishers, e.g. *The Fly and Other Horror Stories* by JOHN ESCOTT for level 4 and E. A. POE's *Seven Stories of Mystery and Horror* by Hueber for level 2–3.

Simplified short stories for young learners

Grade 9–10

The collections edited by MICHAEL CART are very recommendable for teens. For each anthology, he asked ten well-known American children's authors to write about family (*Necessary Noise*), the future (*Tomorrow-*

Cart's short story anthologies for young adults

Chapter 2   Young adult fiction for EFL learners

land), and about love (*Sex and Love*). The stories' lengths vary from 8–46 pages.

Stories about relationships

Two particularly thought-provoking stories in *Necessary Noise* should be mentioned: "Visit", by WALTER DEAN MYERS, is about a father's visit to a son on death row and SONIA SONES' "Dr. Jekyll and Sister Hyde" is a story in verse about a complicated love-hate relationship between two sisters. A humorous story, LOIS LOWRY's "Snowbound", tells how an 18-year-old daughter's new boyfriend is received by the family.

Stories about the future

Various stories about the vision of the future in different periods of time are recounted in *Tomorrowland*. RODMAN PHILBRIK's "The Last Book in the Universe", a tale about a society in which books no longer exist, could complement *Fahrenheit 451*. LOIS LOWRY's "Rage" and JACQUELINE WOODSON's "The Other Half of Me" are set around the turn of the millennium. The girl in "The Other Half of Me", a product of artificial insemination, is looking for her real father.

Stories with unusual formats

A Gathering of Flowers is a compilation of coming-of-age stories written by various ethnic authors. *Am I Blue?* deals with gay and lesbian themes. *Trapped* is a story collection whose central theme of being trapped brought forth very different stories by 13 YA authors. The most unusual tale of *Trapped* is the 14-page story "The Escape" by WALTER DEAN MYERS. It is about a 15-year-old black male's visit to a psychologist, probably set at a juvenile detention center. The short visit is told in two separately printed parts: the left column of the page tells the exterior action, the right side the boy's thoughts and memories of the past. This format can be used very well in the EFL classroom, with each half of the class reading only one column and later filling each other in on the exterior or interior details. Another good story from the collection is "Minimum Wage" by 28-year-old APPOLLO. It tells the story of a 13-year-old who travels from the Florida sugar cane fields to a big city, gets mugged, and as a homeless with no financial means is lured into the house of a pimp who wants to abuse him. LOIS DUNCAN's own contribution is no horror tale, as usual, but a series of poems she wrote while growing up.

Stories about love and sex

In the *Sex and Love* anthology, the story "Secret Shelf" can be especially recommended. It is a lyrical account of a teenage girl's fixation with sex.

Stories of suspense

From the 10th grade on, JOYCE CAROL OATES' "Where Are You Going, Where Have You Been?" can be highly recommended. It comprises all important elements of a suspense story: two opposing characters, conflict, horror. It gives the chilling account of teenager Connie being manipulated and seduced by Arnold Friend, who obviously plans to abduct her from home, torture and perhaps kill her. It is as terrifying as

EDGAR ALLAN POE's "horror tales", only the events are more likely to happen in real life.

Reluctant readers
The short stories for younger learners can also be used for reluctant readers.

Boys' stories – girls' stories?
For male readers, HOROWITZ's *Horror Stories* collection can be recommended. Children's author JON SCIESZKA has edited *Guys Write For Guys Read*, a compilation of very short short stories written by male authors specifically for boys and reluctant readers. On SCIESZKA's website guys-read.com, recommendations for boys' books are given, many of which are funny, adventurous, or scary books. Another short story collections for boys could be *Ultimate Sports*.

> **TIP**
> Ask your students to create their own ghost and horror stories and collect them in a nicely bound book with a well-designed cover.
> Story beginnings like "It was a dark and silly night" can trigger all kinds of ideas. You can also show them a sequence of pictures from the Spiegelman & Mouly book and have learners write texts to the pictures.

12 Verse novels

Verse novels are narratives in poetic form, which have exploded in popularity. The form reflects not only the variety of narrative forms employed by children's authors, but it is also meant to attract the not-so-avid readers because lines are shorter and the story can be read more quickly.

Appeal and advantage of verse novels for young readers

Verse novels differ considerably in style concerning line length, the use of imagery, and language level. The language in CREECH's and WOODSON's novels written for younger children is far less complex, although not simple. HERRICK's verse novels have much shorter lines and therefore can be read faster than *Out of the Dust*, in which HESSE – due to its content – emphasizes imagery and rhythm. FROST combines these elements and adds another one: form. *The Braid* and *Diamond Willow*, for example, are intent on using shapes that fit the stories and the themes.
There is no limit to genres written in verse form; thus verse novels exist as problem novels, adventure stories, historical narratives, and even as information books.

Variety of verse novels

Chapter 2   Young adult fiction for EFL learners

Recommendations for the secondary classroom
Grade 5–7

SHARON CREECH: *Love That Dog*

This is the story of a boy learning to enjoy writing his own poetry. The teacher motivates her students to write poetry using models from well-known American poets. One of these authors is Walter Dean Myers, the award-winning black writer, who honors the school and shows his respect for the students' work. The more the boy is exposed to poetry the more he enjoys it. He also starts to write and design shape poems, which are hung on the classroom wall:

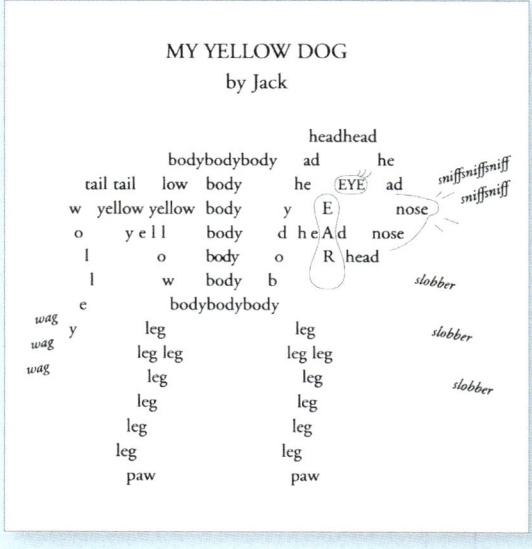

Grade 6–8

JACQUELINE WOODSON: *Locomotion*

As *Love that Dog*, this book involves a teacher making the protagonist write his own poems. He does so reluctantly, but what comes out is a secret that has been locked up deep inside the boy: the house fire that killed his parents. Slowly his childhood as a black kid in his New York foster home and the painful separation from his sister are revealed.

Grade 9–10

This unusual teenage novel gives insight into the hard life of the 12–14-year-old Oklahoma farm girl Billie Jo through her own free verse diary entries. Billie Jo and her family barely manage to stay alive in the raging dust storms of the 1930s, which followed the Stock Market Crash in 1929. The "Dust Bowl", which affected Oklahoma most of all the Midwestern states, was caused by extensive wheat farming. In the novel, readers get to know more about poor farmers' lives, the weather conditions with its lack of rain and devastating dust storms, the destruction of many small farmers by the banks' policy of "tractoring farmers out", the government's help with Roosevelt's New Deal policy, and the westward migration of thousands of "Okies", who were not welcomed by Californians.

Readers get to know this through the eyes of Billie Jo, who suffers from all the hardships although she does not understand everything. Her suffering seems to culminate in her mother's death and her own severe burns on her hands, which make her stop playing the piano, her only joy.

When the drought and the storms and her father's silence after her mother's death become too hard for her to bear, she – like so many Oklahoma families – leaves for California. On the way she meets one of the migrants Woody Guthrie sings about in his *Dust Bowl Songs*, a man who has left his family and steals food from her. She learns that she needs her home to live and therefore returns. The story ends on a note of hope: Billie Jo takes up playing the piano again and her father makes plans for future crops that will prevent the soil erosion which caused the Oklahoma Dust Bowl. Good illustrated information about the period is given by the non-fiction children's book *Children of the Dust Bowl* and by HAMILTON's picture book *DryLongso*. The annotated version is accompanied by a teacher's guide that focuses on intercultural learning (cf. HESSE 2002b).

KAREN HESSE:
Out of the Dust
The Great Depression and the Oklahoma Dust Bowl

Reluctant readers

The Simple Gift, written from the alternating point of view of the three (male, female) main characters, is a novel about homelessness. Sixteen-year-old Billy runs away from a dysfunctional home and jumps a freight train. Away from home, he finds friends who complement and help each other.

The story is written in very short free verse sentences and is therefore not hard to read. Even reluctant readers might find it interesting to read it quickly.

STEVEN HERRICK:
The Simple Gift

Chapter 2   Young adult fiction for EFL learners

Books for boys – books for girls

STEVEN HERRICK: *by the river*

> The verse novel *by the river* deals with growing up in a poor Australian environment. It is especially good for male reluctant readers, since readers can understand the whole story without having to read every page. Fights among boys and adults are frequent, but sometimes they result in friendship.

VIRGINIA EUWER WOLFF: *True Believer*

> EUWER WOLFF's *True Believer*, set in an inner city area of violence and drug abuse, appears to be more of a girls' book. In her narrative poem, a sequel to *Make Lemonade*, 15-year-old La Vaughn gives an account of all her fears: from sexuality and rape to religion. Her main goal is to escape poverty by getting an education. The title refers to her friends who join a religious fundamentalist group and separate themselves from their best friend until they realize at the end that their "church" has tried to abuse them.

Information through verse novels

All other books in the category "verse novels" seem appropriate for both boys and girls, even though the protagonists may be female. *Out of the Dust*, despite its focus on insightful feelings, is a very informative book that gives readers an idea of the hard life of the 1930s and can very well be used for intercultural learning (see chapter 3,1).

> *Read one of the easier verse novels yourself. Stop the time. Estimate how long your students will take to read it. Try it out with individual students first, for book reports. Find out how much they liked it.*
> *Show one verse novel to your fellow teachers and study their reactions. Often you will find that teachers are afraid of the poetic form, since they seem to have been "tortured" with poetry at school!*

13 A note on poetry, drama and non-fiction

Poetry

Why poetry as a separate literary genre has been left out

Apart from verse novels, poetry has been left out in this book since extensive reading of longer, fictional texts is the focus. Reading relatively short poetry requires different strategies than reading long, fictional texts. Understanding poetry is based on intensive reading, in which every single word has to be understood. Reading long texts may sometimes require intensive reading, too, if core pages have to be comprehended (see chapter 3), but on the whole, extensive reading strategies are to be practiced and applied.

This does not mean that poetry as a children's literature genre is to be neglected in Young Adult literature. On the contrary, it is a very central part. All secondary literature works dealing with children's literature include children's poetry as well (cf. ANDERSON 2006, BUSHMAN & PARKS 2003, NODELMAN & REIMER, NÜNNING & SURKAMP 2006, THALER 2008). From a teaching standpoint, it is even easier to use poetry in the EFL classroom since many poems are so short that working with them – even when using a creative approach – can be done in one single lesson. Especially children's poetry offers a vast range of themes relevant to children. Children's poetry anthologies consist of all kinds of funny and serious poetry: For example, *The Random House Book of Poetry for Children*, edited by children's poet JACK PRELUTSKY and illustrated by American artist ARNOLD LOBEL, covers all kinds of themes from nature to nonsense. Some of the teaching methods often used with poetry in creative writing classes can also be applied to longer texts (see chapter 3).

Drama

Drama as a separate genre has been left out here for the same reason that poetry as a separate art form has been omitted. There is no doubt: drama is a very important genre in the literary classroom, and especially well-suited for active learners since plays are to be performed (cf. NÜNNING & SURKAMP 2006: 142). "Unlike children's fiction and children's poetry, in which the role of the child is primarily that of reception and response ..., children's drama ... places the child in the role of 'writer' and performer" (WATSON 216).

Why drama as a separate literary genre has been left out

Although drama has been left out in this book on fiction, it plays an important role as a teaching approach. Chapters 3 and 4 will focus on play-acting as a major method to encourage students' individual and collective responses to prose texts. Students' interpretations will be mirrored in dramatized texts, written role profiles, speeches, and acted-out scenes. With drama techniques, language skills are to be practiced and improved. In *Mittelstufe* classrooms, and especially with weaker learners, drama activities have a great potential.

Applied drama techniques in the reading classroom

> **TIP**
> *If you are interested in using poetry and drama in the active, creative EFL classroom, research the variety of methods and approaches that Nünning & Surkamp 2006 present. If you are looking for plays to be used for younger and weaker students, you should find shorter texts and one-act plays in all German educational publishers' catalogues.*

Non-fiction

Although this book is concerned with fiction, I have included the following chapter on non-fiction to pay tribute to the large number of readers who are not "literary readers". Why should reading literacy be acquired only through the fine arts, which the American poll *Reading at Risk*

The exclusion of non-fiction in reading literacy surveys

Chapter 2   Young adult fiction for EFL learners

(NATIONAL ENDOWMENT FOR THE ARTS 2004) would have us believe? Why should reading newspapers, magazines, and non-fiction books that provide information on a wide range of knowledge domains not be part of a reading literacy survey? In the 2008 American poll, the results of which were published in 2009 under the title *Reading on the Rise*, the reading of electronic sources was finally part of the questionnaire (cf. NATIONAL ENDOWMENT FOR THE ARTS 2009).

In spite of this book's focus on fiction, I want to acknowledge and support the large number of non-fiction readers or even "non-readers", many of whom are males (cf. WILHELM 2002, SAX 2006). With this chapter, I want to emphasize that there is a very large variety of information books on the market which are well worth reading and are excellent sources for gaining literacy.

Definition of non-fiction

Information books are also called "non-fiction" or "factual books". These are texts "specifically designed in print, graphics and illustrations to interest, inform and instruct young people about subjects, events and ideas they encounter" in their young lives (WATSON 368).

Wide range of information books

Information books cover a wide range of texts, reference books such as dictionaries and encyclopedias, topic books about science, history, geography etc. (resource books), (auto-) biography, travel books, how-to books etc. In the 1980s and 1990s, British publishing companies Usborne and Dorling Kindersley had a big impact on international non-fiction publishing with its colorful illustrations and overall design (cf. WATSON: 368ff).

Design and style as means of informing and entertaining

In presenting "hard facts", design and narrative are important, especially in a visual culture and with competing electronic media. Publishers use many more illustrations, bigger letters, and different type faces to motivate readers. Books have to be made entertaining so that information and instruction are closely linked. Nowadays, publishers often apply both forms of media simultaneously. For example, the very popular original print medium, the *Magic School Bus* series (1986), eventually grew into an animated video series that takes learners on field trips anywhere between the deep sea and outer space. Through more interactive forms of games, CD-ROMS, and websites, the terms "instructive" and "entertaining" are beginning to overlap (cf. PAUL in ZIPES 1: 187f.).

Narrative

Not only the design is important, but so is the narrative. Often "hard facts" are presented in story form. For example, PAUL FLEISCHMAN's *Townsend Warbler*, which is about the Western bird, tells the story of explorer Townsend's encounters with the bird that carries his name. DAVID MACAULY's architectural books are actually works of fiction based on "hard" architectural facts.

A subset of information books is the group of how-to books, which according to SMITH & WILHELM (2002), especially reluctant readers tend to use because reading and action are closely connected. Dorling Kindersley offers a wide range of how-to books, from how to draw to how to build cars. An especially interesting how-to book is JANE BULL's *Make It*, a book on making all kinds of items from scratch.

How-to books

In some information books, facts are also presented in humorous form, like in DEARY's & BROWN's *Horrible History* series. *The Magic School Bus* series is now also available in comic form. DAVID MACAULY's *The Way Things Work* combines information with funny cartoons.

Humor in non-fiction

Since the 1970s, biographies have appeared in abundance with raised standards and a new frankness for children. The genre received great attention when FREEDMAN's *Lincoln, a Photobiography* received the Newbery Medal in 1987. Watson calls this biography "a book as strongly written and emotionally compelling as a novel" (82). However, at the same time Watson warns readers to examine the representation of facts critically. Too often biographies tend to be inaccurate; they are carelessly researched by authors using unreliable data; they tend to over-simplify and glorify in order to teach; they apply too many taboos leaving out unwanted facts (82).

Biography

Recommendations for the secondary classroom
Grade 6–8

> MORDICAI GERSTEIN's Caldecott Medal-winning picture book is a most extraordinary story of Philippe Petit, a man who walked on a tightrope between the two towers of the World Trade Center in New York City on August 7, 1974. The story is even more outstanding today after the fall of the Twin Towers.
> Two films which have appeared since then could be used together with the picture book for older and younger audiences: a 10-minute animated film (2003) and the 2008 documentary *Man on Wire*.

MORDICAI GERSTEIN: The Man Who Walked Between the Towers

> Like other books in the *Coming to America* series (about German, Irish, Italian, Japanese, and Vietnamese Immigrants), *Why Mexican Immigrants Came to America* was written as a very easy illustrated graded reader. The series may be especially good for 7th grades and *Hauptschule*.
> LeeAnne Gelletly wrote a similar series for more advanced students.

LEWIS K. PARKER: Why Mexican Immigrants Came to America

Chapter 2   Young adult fiction for EFL learners

Grade 9–10

Rob Shone & Nick Spender: *Rosa Parks*

> The graphic biography depicts Rosa Parks' life from childhood to adulthood, when she refused to give up her bus seat to a white man. The easy-to-read cartoon-like book is accompanied by information on the Jim Crow laws and pioneer times. A glossary is included at the end. Parks' courage and long-lasting commitment to the cause of civil rights for blacks is depicted in heavy strokes and stark colors.

Carole Boston Weatherford: *Birmingham, 1963*

> This 40-page story about the conflict during the US Civil Rights Movement written in poems by black poet Boston Weatherford informs young readers about the struggles against racism.

Luiz Rodriguez: *Always Running*

> This autobiographical account of growing up in different ethnic communities should be especially interesting for migrant teenagers and young adults. Luiz Rodriguez' rather long *Always Running* is about the difficulties of growing up as immigrants in the USA in the 1960s. Rodriguez, a man of Mexican descent, candidly tells of his problems and his own violent behavior, which even resulted in gang life and crime. Reading excerpts in class might motivate individual students to read the whole volume.

Reluctant readers

Graphic information books

The graphic biography series and the DK readers series about Star Wars seem to be especially attractive for "non-readers". The graphic biography *Sitting Bull* is a very motivating description of Sitting Bull's fight for his fellow Native Americans.

For more interesting books, turn to the two picture books by Lawrence in the historical fiction chapter 2.5.

Boys' books – girls' books

Children's authors' biographies

Autobiographies of well-known children's authors such as Roald Dahl (*Boy; Going Solo*) and Walter Dean Myers (*Bad Boy*) may be interesting for boys, especially for those who have problems with authority figures. Lowry's beautifully designed and illustrated "book of memories" *Looking Back* might be well-suited for girls. The large number of good, mostly illustrated biographies make it hard to decide on one recommendation.

13 A note on poetry, drama and non-fiction

> **TIP**
>
> Apply the 10 criteria for a good information book (Watson: 369) to any teenage information book that you know:
> - Attractiveness
> - Accuracy
> - Authority
> - Appropriateness
> - Rhetoric
> - Stereotypes
> - Tone
> - Cautions
> - Format
> - Book design

3 Young adult fiction for foreign language development

1 Intercultural communicative competence

**ICC
Intercultural Communicative Competence**

The Common European Framework of Reference (CEFR) describes intercultural communicative competence (ICC) as the main goal of foreign language learning. When learners are learning a second or a foreign language, they are already competent in their mother tongue and its culture. The linguistic and cultural competences concerning each language are modified "by knowledge of the other and contribute to intercultural awareness, skills, and know-how. They enable the individual to develop an enriched, more complex personality and an enhanced capacity for further language learning and greater openness to new cultural experiences" (CEFR 2001: 43). This is more a vision than a goal, but nevertheless everybody involved in language teaching is striving to realize this vision.

The learner as "intercultural speaker"

The ideal ICC learner is not supposed to imitate a native speaker as best he/she can, but is supposed to become an "intercultural speaker", "someone who is able to see and establish relationships between languages and cultures" (BYRAM 1999: 364).

While reading authentic YA literature in an EFL context, learners are generally confronted with another culture. Literature, especially fiction, involves readers much more than textbooks can or information texts aim to do. The texts, mostly about young persons whose lives are endangered by outside forces, ask readers to engage with the protagonists. They help them to sympathize with other people, maybe distance themselves from their own lives, but they may also lead readers to distance themselves from the characters' lives. In any case, readers may get a better understanding of the other and of themselves (cf. BREDELLA & DELANOY 15).

The intercultural reader's response

Reading YA texts allows for an intercultural exchange that is more meaningful to learners than reading about the invented lives of the textbook families. Textbook texts pretend they deal with "real life". But learners know that the texts are written for the purpose of learning the language.

Therefore, YA literature offers a great opportunity to involve learners with fictional texts, with texts that do not pretend they are "real". They are the invention of specific authors. Authors themselves are "products" of the foreign cultures. They can only recount what they know, what they have experienced, what they have researched from sources coming from the cultural setting. The stories we are dealing with are mostly written in the foreign language for native speakers, most of whom share their culture with the authors.

Reading leads learners to experience foreign cultures and value systems, which they learn about on the basis of their own cultural experiences and value system. And thus they negotiate the meaning between the foreign cultures represented in the text and start to understand the other culture (cf. BREDELLA & DELANOY: 15).

Readers most likely begin to feel with the characters and better understand their motives and aims. Adopting different perspectives through reading literature is necessary for social interaction in real life as well (cf. BREDELLA 2002; NÜNNING & SURKAMP 2006: 28).

The effect of reading is not always as immediately visible as in the following example: While discussing the novels *La Línea* and *Crossing the Wire* with students in a YA literature class at an American university, one student said that the novels helped her to understand Latinos better. Before reading about Hispanics' difficulties, they bothered her in her Floridian environment and she would have liked to send them back to where they came from. After reading the novels, she started reflecting about the lives of these immigrants and decided to tutor a Mexican child in reading English.

Immediate reader response

In general, as teachers we should not expect such immediate attitudinal changes among our learners. Otherwise we would be right in just using didactic literature that tells youngsters "how to be good". Fiction, especially stories that are not so easily comprehensible, may prepare learners for the "normality of the strange" (*"Normalität des Fremden"*) around us (HUNFELD 2004). With this term, HUNFELD refers to the fact that everyone has to get used to living in a modern-day multicultural society. Learners learn this not only by being exposed to strangers, but also by being exposed to the strangeness of literature. Therefore, HUNFELD also calls literature a "foreign language" (*"Fremdsprache Literatur"*; cf. 2004: 373ff.).

The strangeness of literature

Since all authentic texts are written in the "otherness" of the foreign language, all literature genres, not only multicultural texts dealing with minority protagonists, appear suitable for intercultural learning. Any good piece of literature poses riddles to readers. It raises questions and does not answer them without the reader's active contribution. Therefore, it offers students a chance to fill the gaps (*Leerstellen*), to use their imagination based on their own experiences.

The Giver is not a multicultural novel, and yet I consider it highly suitable for intercultural learning. It is set completely in the future, in a "secondary", imagined fantasy world in which the reality we know no longer exists. It does not focus on a child of ethnic minority, and yet it is stranger than some multicultural novels. This work of fantasy poses all kinds of questions; initially it is full of riddles, even for native speakers. But it is exactly this aspect of literature, the aspect of literature as "a foreign language", that provides a basis for intercultural learning. Engaging with the strange world of the novel, readers question their own societies. They ask themselves whether our society is similar to the one *The Giver*'s community has gotten rid of; or is it the society in which they live? They learn about social engineering and ask themselves if this

Intercultural learning with a fantasy novel

is possible in the world they are living in. The two societies described or hinted at represent two very different political cultures! ==A book must make readers wonder to make communication meaningful.== (cf. also chapter 4).

Intercultural learning via email exchanges

The novel is also good for intercultural learning in another respect. It is read in almost every American school and in many countries worldwide. Thus there are lots of opportunities to get involved in email contact with other schools, both American and international. Students will see how differently the novel can be received by other cultures and thus they will be able to negotiate meaning with participants from the other culture (cf. MÜLLER-HARTMANN 1999: 173ff.). As MÜLLER-HARTMANN & SCHOCKER-V. DITFURTH (2004: 109ff.) point out when citing email contact between American and German students, the reception of books in two different cultures may be very different.

Intercultural learning through contact with the author

Contact to authors, too, which can be made through publishers, will give learners another great opportunity for intercultural learning.

When researching the reception of *The Giver* in the USA, students will learn that it has caused a lot of concern, mostly among fundamentalist parents, about all kinds of issues in various school districts. The way suicide and euthanasia are treated in the book helped it reach No. 11 on the American Library Association's list of most challenged books of the 1990s (cf. USA TODAY 07/20/2001)!

Intercultural learning through multicultural literature

Multicultural literature, however, works well when migrant learners are involved. ANN JARAMILLO, author of *La Línea*, says her middle school Mexican students are happy to be able to relate to the characters in the book (cf. HESSE 2008).

This is supported by a German university student of Vietnamese origin: when reading Indian-American literature in class she said she was amazed and happy to see how well she could identify with the protagonists described in the short story collection *Interpreter of Maladies* by JUMPHA LAHIRI. She added that she would have liked to have read more multicultural literature at her German high school.

> **TIP** *Think about which texts would be most suitable for intercultural learning in a class that you have taught/are teaching? If you have many migrant teens in your class, try to find out if they want literature dealing with their own culture of origin. Not every child wants to be confronted with it!*

2 Tasks and teachers

1 Tasks

Tasks have a specific meaning in EFL teaching based on the task-based language learning (TBLL) theory, which has been prevalent since the 1980s, and which has heavily influenced the CEFR. Nunan (1989: 10) defines the task as a piece of classroom practice involving *"learners in comprehending, manipulating, producing or interacting in the target language while their attention is principally focused on meaning rather than on form."* This does not mean that form (correctness) is unimportant, but form has a service function: to support communication. Willis (1996: 23) emphasizes the role of activities with a visible outcome. Candlin (2003: 42) calls classrooms "places where particular kinds of interaction occur and are situated, and where participants enact a range of mutually involving roles and work towards achieving particular personal and group purposes." Tasks should be designed according to the basic question: "who does what with whom, on what content, with what resources, when, how, and why? (Breen 1987:30).

Due to the task-based approach and the reader response theory, both of which put interaction into the center of teaching and learning, literature has become firmly established in the EFL classroom (cf. Bredella 2000: 376f.).

The task-based approach

As the reader response theory made clear in literature interaction occurs between text and reader. But in the reading classroom the element of group interaction – interaction between many readers and the teacher – is an additional challenge. This challenge can be used to an advantage, as chapters 3–5 show. Legutke & Thomas (1991) identify three major elements in the interactive process: the individual, the group and the theme, all of which maintain a dynamic balance in theme-centered interaction (cf. 169). They emphasize interaction since tasks are affected by group processes involving group anxieties and group rivalries, something that teachers know all to well (cf. Williams & Burden 1997: 170).

The interactive process

In the case of YA literature, motivating literature and motivating tasks go hand in hand to promote learning. Ideally through interaction with literature, complex learner identities are formed (Müller-Hartmann & Schocker-v. Ditfurth 2004: 121); ideally readers reach a "third place" (Kramsch 1993), which frees them from the constraints of everyday life (cf. Delanoy 1999: 145; Benton 1992: 22ff.).

Relationship between readers, tasks, and texts

It is self-evident that in task-based language learning tasks are learner-centered. Tasks are to be planned in such a way that they take teenagers' pre-knowledge seriously and apply what is to be learnt to their knowledge of the world.

Learner-centered tasks

81

Chapter 3 Young adult fiction for foreign language development

The three phases

In the pre-reading phase learners are made curious about the novel and interest is aroused. Book covers, text beginnings, text excerpts, role cards (see chapter 4) are only a few examples of how interest can be created. The while-reading phase takes advantage of young people's wish to understand the text, establish a relationship with the characters, empathize or identify with them, engage in the plot. With tasks that make readers participate in protagonists' lives readers start to feel with characters and become ready to change perspectives. Many of the creative activities listed below are to help young readers feel with the novels' characters. In the post-reading phase learners relate their views to the ones of the protagonists, compare, contrast, review what characters went through on the basis of their own lives.

This three-phase approach has been generally accepted for all literature teaching. MÜLLER-HARTMANN & SCHOCKER-V. DITFURTH (2004: 129) add a transition phase in which readers are made aware of their own lives in their own cultures with their own value systems so that real intercultural learning through reading literature may take place.

Creative literary tasks

Here is a list of action-oriented, learner-centered, creative tasks that are excellent for learners to understand texts, imagine settings and atmosphere, and participate in characters' lives. Today many of the tasks can be found in various literature teaching materials.

Text comphrehension

Comprehending texts
True-false answers
Matching parts of sentences
Multiple choice
"Who says what" statements

Text recreating

Recreating texts
Leaving out text passages to be filled in according to the surrounding text. The gaps to be filled with just single words, phrases, or whole passages.
Jumbled sentences or paragraphs to be put back into the original order.

Text creating

Creating new texts
Writing a new ending, a new beginning, a sequel
Dramatizing prose texts
Condensing parts by leaving out sections that students think too long
Writing poetry using the content and maybe certain words of a prose excerpt or of the whole text
Filling in letters that characters write to other characters
Writing a story from different perspectives (this is worthwhile in order to realize different perspectives, especially if a story is told very one-sidedly).
Turning one subgenre into another one: e.g. writing a rather boring story as a mystery

Visualizing texts
In pictures (sketches, paintings, clippings, photos, posters, advertisements ...)
In mime and gestures
Through bodys work (freeze frames, tableaus)
Through role plays and acting
Through film
Creating hypertexts
Using You Tube

Visualization

Using sound
Reading text passages by using different volumes, tones, pitch and recording them
Making songs for central text passages or the whole text
Singing text passages
Finding music representing atmosphere, characters, the meaning of the whole novel

Representing text in sounds

Responding to texts
Writing letters to characters
Writing letters to the author
Writing reviews
Using email contacts, chat rooms, internet forums to exchange ideas on texts

Responding

In task-based language learning, a work plan is important. It should be published and discussed with learners at the beginning of a teaching unit (task-as-work plan) and may be changed throughout the unit (task-in-progress) (cf. BREEN: 23). The work plan is supposed to be a guideline for both learners and teacher. It shows the breaking up of the novel into sections, the accompanying tasks, and the intended outcome (cf. HESSE 1999: 15ff). Part of such a plan may also be a list of tasks every student has chosen at the beginning of the reading process, so that students can be questioned as experts for certain themes and characters. The plan below is taken from the teacher's guide to *The Giver* (cf. HESSE 1999: 25) and is supposed to accompany the reading and teaching schedule (15ff.).

The task-based work plan

Themes/Tasks	Students' names	To be done by (date)
The community Rules and regulations Ceremonies Landscape, architecture, traffic Citizens' relationships		

Chapter 3   Young adult fiction for foreign language development

Themes/Tasks	Students' names	To be done by (date)
Other communities and the outside world Differences between other communities Elsewhere		
Individual characters – outward appearance, behaviour, feelings, attitudes Jonas Lilly Gabe Mother Father Chief Elder Giver		
Language Official language of the community The real meaning of "release" Core vocabulary		

<small>Fast reading – slow reading; straight – through reading – segmented reading</small>

Here one can see that extensive and intensive reading complement each other. The whole text is read extensively; but the parts informing students about the selected theme or character have to be read intensively. THALER's "straight-through approach" (105) seems to be adequate for advanced readers or be acceptable for really easy texts; however, with the more challenging YA novels like *The Giver*, I strongly recommend the "segment approach" with a good, slow in-class reading introduction, since even for native speakers the novel poses so many riddles in the beginning that intermediate learners of English might find it too demanding to read the whole novel on their own. Later when they are familiarized with the strangeness of the society, they can be asked to read sections on their own. Only for weaker students, who also want to enjoy narrative texts, I support the so-called sandwich approach, which leaves-out chapters or substitutes chapters through summaries or film (THALER 105).

> **TIP** *Complete the list of creative tasks by adding other activities. Put the activities into a ranking order. Think of two YA novels you have read and sketch two teaching units. Which tasks and activities listed above are more appropriate for each text?*

2 Teachers

As one can see, tasks are open, almost project-like lesson units in which a cooperative teacher-learner relationship reigns. Aesthetic reading should provide as much openness as possible so that individual response is made possible and "negotiation of meaning" can occur (DELANOY 147).

Teacher-learner cooperation in negotiating meaning

Teachers are the ones who guide their learners through their learning process. In the literature-based classroom, they take over the role of facilitators, the one who manages interaction by connecting different comments, suggesting different interpretations of ideas, and clarifying positions instead of telling learners how to interpret a story (cf. MÜLLER HARTMANN & SCHOCKER-V. DITFURTH 2004:31).

The teacher as classroom manager

But not all teachers are yet aware of their new role in the reading classroom. The following (shortened) email written by a German high school student to Lois Lowry, the author of *The Giver*, vividly shows how desperate the teacher's prescriptiveness has made the student. The teacher obviously acts against all principles stated above:

A teacher prescribing meaning

Dear Mrs. Lowry,
I am 14 years old and I write from Germany for the following reason: There is a real problem with "The Giver", especially with the end!
I do like it, and many other pupils, too, but not the teachers. They can't deal with it. And they will never accept that it could be a good ending, because, the two boys die, of course, and that's it. And then they're searching for clues and explanations everywhere in the book to prove that the book's end is a really, really bad one ... And they make us to do so, of course.
I tried everything but they don't want to believe that it could also be a good ending and they don't accept me to make up my own one! They just want me to write down what YOUR idea of the ending is like (How do THEY know?) They give marks and stuff like that, bad marks if my idea is different to the teacher's one and good ones if I repeat all the words the teacher said... That seems so strange, because, well, IF it's an open ending I can have my OWN ideas, can't I?
Why do I have to write the teacher's opinion? If he knew more than me about the real ending, all right, but he doesn't! And that's why I ask you to have a word with the teachers. Perhaps it would help if you made it clear, if Jonas and Gabriel die or survive. Just tell the teachers, both boys die and that's it. That's what they want to hear and perhaps they'll stop making us to do that stupid clue finding in the whole book then. It's no fun to go through a book for the third time while thinking "Is that perhaps the sentence that proves Jonas will be dying later? Or is it the next one?" That's boring. And it destroys the joy of reading... There are so many kids in my class that hate the book just because of the way it was

A student trying to interpret the ending her way asks the author for help! She is powerless.

Chapter 3   Young adult fiction for foreign language development

taught! I would hate it, too, if I hadn't read it before.
Perhaps there are other ways ...
But the teachers can't go on like that! They make the students hate books like "The Giver".
Yours hopefully,
Katrin   (name changed)

Young readers may be turned off literature by "prescriptive teaching"

I only know about this email because Lois Lowry forwarded it to me, as the writer of the *The Giver's* teacher's guide (1999); but I do not know how LOWRY responded to it. I wonder how many other teenagers are prescribed what to think! We agree that this is exactly the opposite of what she as a writer and we as teachers want young readers to do. We want readers to think for themselves! This is obviously what the girl had done on her own before the novel was read in class. There are no clues in the book that favor the teacher's interpretation. LOIS LOWRY gets lots of emails asking about the ending (cf. http://www.loislowry.com), but always refers to the text alone saying that she wanted it to have an open end.

The original ending of *The Giver*

Here is the full text of the ending of *The Giver* (136):
[After a dangerous escape from the "community", Jonas and Gabriel, the baby, arrive at the top of a hill; they see houses below.]

> "... and all at once he could see lights, and he recognized them now. He knew they were shining through the windows of rooms, that they were red, blue and yellow lights that twinkled from trees in places where families created and kept memories, where they celebrated love.
> Downward, downward, faster and faster. Suddenly he was aware with certainty and joy that below, ahead, they were waiting for him; and that they were waiting, too, for the baby. For the first time, he heard something that he knew to be music. He heard people singing.
> Behind him, across vast distances of space and time, from the place he had left, he thought he heard music too. But perhaps it was only an echo." (136)

Open endings should be left open

This ending is open to all kinds of interpretations and should be left open. What a chance this teacher missed to have students render their versions of the ending! Creative writing tasks and sharing personal experiences are among the typical TBLL tasks (cf. WILLIS 1996: 26–28; 149–154). The teacher could also have shared his own reading experience with his students, in written or oral form! Writing to one's own students is also a very personal and therefore very effective form of communication.
According to ROGERS' humanistic psychology, which the task-based language learning approach follows, four attitudinal qualities between teacher and students should be regarded:

- emphatic understanding of students' learning processes
- learning from their perspective
- valuing, respecting, and trusting learners
- "realness" of the teacher (cf. LEGUTKE ET AL. 2009: 44f.).

> **TIP**
> Is looking for clues in texts, something which the previously-mentioned teacher has his students do, a bad idea? Give reasons for when it makes sense.

3 Improving "receptive" and "productive" skills

In a communicative classroom it is evident that skills cannot really be taught separately. In such a reading classroom, negotiation about what one has read is to be meaningful for each individual reader. "Receptive skills" of reading and listening, and "productive skills" such as writing, speaking, and mediating are interrelated. Or as CAMERON (2001) puts it: "skills to learn a spoken language" and "literacy skills" (reading and writing different texts) are not to be separated. "Receptive" and "productive" skills are put in quotation marks because neither skill is only fully receptive. A lot of active brain work is needed for the supposedly "receptive" skills of reading and listening.

According to the CEFR, the term "competences" is more comprehensive than the term "skills" as it comprises "the sum of knowledge, skills and characteristics" that allows a person to perform actions (cf. COUNCIL OF EUROPE 2001: 9). However, I will use the traditional term "skills" since many textbooks and much teaching literature are still based on skills.

The four skills interacting with each other

1 Reading

Skill 1 in a reading classroom is of course reading, in this case reading longer texts than those in general course books. Numbers of pages cannot be used here to define extensive reading. Extensive reading may range from a few pages of a short story to a voluminous novel. In the case of the intermediate reading classroom, however, I tried to limit the volume to about 200(+) pages, with many novels being much shorter. Since reading comprehension is the basic goal without which no other goals can be reached, extensive reading strategies must be practiced so that they will be applied automatically at a later stage.

Reading strategies for extensive reading

Reading comprehension

The good message of the 2001 OECD "PISA" study is that reading motivation can be supported in school and reading strategies can very well be trained (DEUTSCHES PISA-KONSORTIUM 2001: 129ff.). Good readers usually apply reading strategies automatically (cf. UR 1996: 148);

Practicing reading strategies with slow readers

but beginning readers, slow readers, and EFL learners often have to be taught to read longer texts efficiently which means quickly, appropriately, and skillfully (cf. UR: 147). Unfortunately, intensive reading is still the dominant form of reading in the German EFL classroom and is mainly practiced with short texts in course book. This has produced a teaching method that wants learners to know every single "new" word in pre-reading activities in order to be able to understand a text based on its context.

Reading strategies

Word formation

If one believes our university students who frequently say they never read longer stories, let alone novels, until advanced grades in the *Oberstufe*, one can conclude that many learners in intermediate grades are not at all used to extensive reading. Therefore, the first few reading lessons should be reserved for reactivating students' knowledge of word formation. This can be done with a competitive activity such as finding as many words as possible which are derived from a root word. Thus prefixes and suffixes will get used again in a playful, competitive way. Vocabulary expansion might become fun as students recognize they know more words than previously expected. Something that is often observed in American reading classrooms could be copied in German classrooms as well: on a separate wall, cards with all suffixes and prefixes (with their semantic meaning) are listed in different colors. Learners could position word stems and word beginnings and endings in such a way that even poetry-like forms (in lines, repetitions, rhyme …) could be arranged.

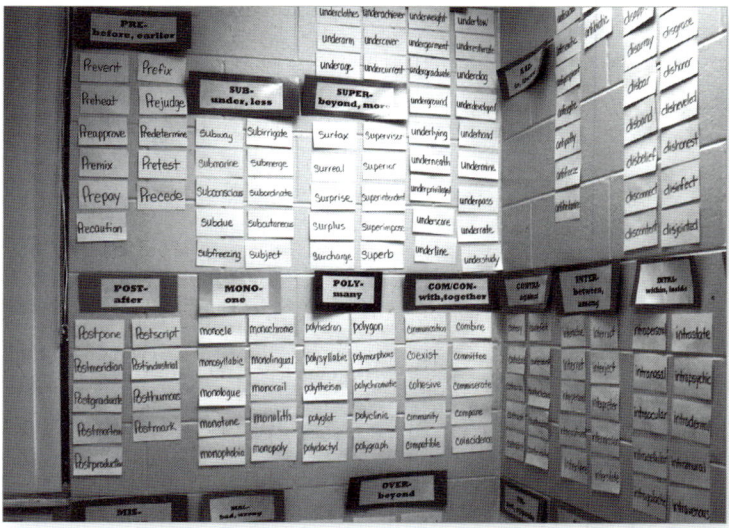

American reading classroom

Being able to apply reading strategies automatically is necessary to improve one's reading speed. The pre-, while-, and post-reading strategies in the box below may have to be included in learners' first extensive reading practice. The focus should still be on content and students should not always be made aware of the reading strategies that they are applying (cf. GLATZLE ET AL. 2006).

Pre-reading strategies
- **Predicting to trigger reading motivation:**
Predicting what the story may be about based on the book cover, a text excerpt, or prefabricated role cards about characters.

While-reading strategies
- **Predicting, visualizing, problem solving**
Constant prediction about how the story may continue; visualization of events, characters, setting … (Active readers do this constantly, trying to follow the clues the authors give to solve a problem, predict the outcome. (cf. UR 148)
- **Skimming: reading, listening for gist**
Acquiring a global understanding of what is happening
- **Scanning: reading for detail**
Retrieving specific information
- **Inferring word meaning**
Inferring meaning without using a dictionary based on the context, from the knowledge of other languages, from word formation rules, from the sound of words
- **Inferring text meaning**
Reading between the lines, interpreting images …
- **Knowledge of text types and structure of certain text types (newspapers, magazines, novels, letters …)**
This may be important to be able to differentiate between fiction and non-fiction, to understand the purpose of various novel types (i.e. letter novels, multi-perspective novels, lyrical novels …)

Post-reading strategies
- **Reflection, interpretation, analyzing, summarizing, reviewing**
Analytical and critical reflection; summarizing, reviewing characters' values, standpoints, reviewing the whole novel
- **Transfer**
Transferring events, ideas, philosophies onto other situations, reviewing one's own standpoint

Chapter 3 — Young adult fiction for foreign language development

> **TIP**
> Look at the box in Penny Ur's "A Course in Language Teaching" (148) titled "Efficient and Inefficient Reading" and identify reading strategies that your students are lacking.
> Design tasks that help these students to catch up with efficient readers.
> Use Ur's recommendations (149) as help.

2 Listening

Listening to the novel on CD

Whereas students can read sections of the novel at home, a tape or CD is still most often in the hands of the teacher, and therefore listening is mainly practiced at school. More and more educational publishers make CDs accessible and affordable now, so that books (in print) are also accompanied by audio CDs. Listening in the reading classroom is predominantly aimed at listening to the spoken text, which is normally read by just one actor/actress. Therefore it may be even more complex than listening to a dramatized version of the written text (in drama or film). The disadvantage of listening to reading is that the listener has to concentrate very hard in order to catch as much as he/she can during the limited listening time if the oral text is not accompanied by a written text that can be consulted again later.

Listening strategies

Therefore, it may be wise to practice listening at first with the help of the written text. In this case, listening supports understanding: the way a text is read, how the speaker/narrator uses his voice to imitate female and male, old and young people, humans and animals, the pauses, the tone of voice, the reading speed, and accent(s). All of this supports understanding and should help learners comprehend a text better, to even realize nuances (humor, satire…), which are hard to grasp from just printed letters on paper. Once learners have overcome initial difficulties with the written text, just listening to certain passages (without reading the text) is recommended in order to focus on listening only.

Listening tasks: scanning and skimming

Listening is easier for a learner if the listener knows what kind of information he/she is supposed to look for (scanning) or whether he/she is supposed to listen for gist only (skimming). Therefore, tasks should be clarified before listening. Listening twice may also be appropriate, listening for gist the first time and for specific details the second time. As listeners' minds tend to wander, tasks should be accompanied by note-taking or worksheets. Worksheets meant to just test learners' listening comprehension should not involve writing.

While-listening comprehension

To test while-listening comprehension, the following exercise formats are useful:
- multiple choice
- right-wrong statements
- matching halves of sentences
- putting sentences or pictures into order
- visualization involving drawing
- matching pictures with sentences

Testing learners' listening comprehension

Pre-listening

For pre-listening, pictures leading into the topic are useful.

Pre-listening tasks

Post-listening

For post-listening, body work exercises, such as tableaus or freeze-frames, which mirror students' comprehension and interpretation, can be applied.

Post-listening tasks

The focus on in-class presentations nowadays demands a lot of listening. To make sure students are really listening, some note-taking or evaluating tasks may be helpful so that the presentations can be discussed later.

Listening to classmates' presentations

In a reading classroom in which communication about the content of a text is the most important part and students are actively involved in their own reading response, the classroom is a forum for their interpretations, their gap-filling, their creation of new texts (see this chapter on writing). Here, listening is closely connected to speaking, and speaking is again closely connected to the writing that learners have done.

Listening to classmates' and teacher's attempts at meaning-making

> **TIP**
> Always use pre-listening tasks to prepare learners for the actual listening tasks. Explain to the students exactly what they are going to hear and what specifically they are supposed to find out. Break longer texts up into sections so that students can respond after every break (cf. Ur 108).

3   Speaking

For communication about issues in a novel, many tasks have the potential to make learners communicate through speaking and listening. Here, students are encouraged to speak about their responses to the text following motivating tasks that were previously given, so that individual responses are discussed. This leads to a better understanding of classmates' ideas and most likely, of the text itself.

There are many ways in which interesting, meaningful class discussions can be prepared involving interesting tasks and a variety of interactive forms.

Communicating in the classroom

Chapter 3   Young adult fiction for foreign language development

Making speaking meaningful: Speaking about individual tasks

Labor division gives communication purpose

For example, if the setting of *Out of the Dust* is to be discussed in class, students could have been asked (while listening to the CD) to underline all lines expressing where and when the story takes place. Division of labor works best because then, listening to others really makes sense. Some students might have been asked to underline the weather situation while others were to research the political situation during the Great Depression in the Oklahoma Panhandle. The same can be expanded into homework: different groups are asked to research the geography, the climate, the economy, and the political situation. Everybody brings their research results to class and the jigsaw puzzle pieces of the situation in this state in the 1930s are put together.

Speaking about interpretations

Speaking about readers' reading between the lines

The above task seems rather easy since the setting in a historical novel is based on facts, whereas the plot itself and the characters are created by the author. When discussing character traits, not only are individual characters interesting but relationships are as well. The question of what kind of family Billie Jo was born into is an interesting question since the verse novel is basically a historical family story. Also, her perspective as a first-person narrator telling the story in diary entries is an issue that needs closer observation. I will only give one example from the very beginning of the novel which can lead to all kinds of interpretation questions. Here a passage has to be read "intensively", since in such a case readers are to understand every word. With this word knowledge, learners still have to "read between the lines". They have to visualize and interpret what it means when Billie Jo writes she has "cheekbones like bicycle handles" (2002: 7); or when at the very beginning of the novel, Billie Jo retells the story of her birth that she must have heard from her mother many times before:

"Ma crouched,
barefoot, bare bottomed
over the swept floor
because that's where Daddy said it'd be best." (7)

Taking over characters' perspectives

Reading between the lines means seeing in one's mind's eye that Billie Jo was born on a kitchen floor that had been previously swept clean by Billie Jo's mother herself. Questions like these are triggered: Was her mother a very responsible woman? Or was she scared of the birth, of possible infections? Was her husband the one to give her advice or even orders on where to give birth to the child? Is he the one in charge? Does she always follow the rules that he sets?

Speaking in cooperative forms

Speaking about this in class does not always have to be teacher-centered but can be substituted by many cooperative forms in which every student has an active part. Plenary discussions should be used mainly to summarize and to discuss general issues following other interactive forms or for introduction purposes. Every practicing teacher knows that in plenary discussions – without previous thinking, writing, and speaking activities – a small number of students do all the talking and the rest of the class either listens, does not listen, or just repeats what has already been said. Since plenary talks, in which one person – mainly the teacher – does the speaking, is the predominant activity in German classrooms, I would like to present other, interactive speaking activities involving every participant.

Speaking can be organized in a variety of cooperative forms so that every member of the class is involved. Cooperative classrooms are often praised for their equalitarian, democratic potential (cf. KESSLER 1992). Not only does cooperative learning give everybody the chance to contribute individual ideas, but it is also more effective since everybody can practice simultaneously.

Plenary speaking activities
Double circles

This speaking activity using two big circles is a very effective method. In this activity, the whole class is split into two groups sitting in two circles, an inner and an outer circle, facing each other. Each member of the inner circle talks with a member of the outer circle. After some time, one circle rotates so that new partners are found. Specific tasks previously given to members of each circle are discussed. Students take notes and inform their next partner after one circle has rotated again. Learners should not move more than three times.

Activities involving each individual

Whole class moving *(Marktplatz)*

Equipped with a worksheet containing one task or a collection of tasks, learners can move freely in the room, interview various classmates, and fill in their worksheets with their answers. Everybody must interview three classmates!

Everybody talking at the same time

Chorus chanting

Chorus speaking seems an old-fashioned form of teaching. In former times, results had to be read from the board together. Today, this seems a boring, almost embarrassing activity of mere reproduction.

Chorus speaking, however, can be fun if the speech is rhythmic. It works with call-and-response exercises in which, like in jazz chants, the teacher, a student, or one group calls out a sentence and the other students repeat it in the same rhythm. This is done in poetry slams, which are popular among many young people. Why not use sentences from a book, speak them in any kind of rhythm, and let the others repeat them?

Speaking together in chants

Chapter 3   Young adult fiction for foreign language development

Activities involving pairs and small groups

Small group speaking activities
Think, pair, share
Pair conversations are another very effective form. These involve pairing up two students, each of whom had different tasks to fulfill at school or at home. This is the least threatening social activity in which a comfortable target language atmosphere prevails (cf. MÜLLER-HARTMANN & SCHOCKER-V. DITFURTH 2004: 63). Later on, groups of two can be paired with other groups of two to form a new group with a new task. This very easy partner check can also be used to check each other's homework.

Activities involving groups of 4–6 members

Group puzzles and expert groups
This group work involves everybody in two different groups. At first, each individual in a group (A, B, C, D) gets a task and tries to solve the problem alone. Then he/she discusses it with his/her own group. Later, student A1 meets with student B1, C1, and D1 in another group and they compare their answers. In a third stage, they go back to their initial groups and discuss and summarize their results.

Role play to lead into a novel

Role play in small groups with identical tasks
Another way to have everyone speak at once is based on role cards, which can be a good lead-in to a new novel. In the case of *Abomination*, a class of 30 forms six groups with five members each. Each group member gets one of the role cards created by the teacher in advance. On the basis of what each group member has read, they introduce themselves to the other members, become aware of and ask about relationships, and predict what the story may be about. This method can be used for rather enigmatic stories such as Swindells' *Abomination* with the questions of what "Abomination" is, what kind of family he/she/it is living with, and what the friendship between Martha and Scott is like.

Example: *Abomination* role cards

> **Martha Dewhurst**
> schoolgirl; hides from her mother that she is bullied at school, hates her name, since kids turn it into all kinds of nicknames. Martha doesn't like the clothes her mother makes for her since she feels they don't look right. When Scott, a new boy at her school, first arrived, Martha thought he would be her friend, but she realizes that he chases (runs after) her too like everybody else. When she comes home from school, she does not get to eat right away but has to feed something called "Abomination" that's living in the cellar. She hates this task.

3 Improving "receptive" and "productive" skills

Scott
new boy at the school; is put at Martha's table in the classroom and is friendly to her as he lends her his ruler. But the other kids make fun of him and warn him about her. After school he chases (runs after) Martha home calling her Raggedy-Ann, Raggedy-Ann like ten other boys. Simon, his friend, started to chase her so Scott does it too.

Mrs Dewhurst
does not like her daughter to run. Reacts to her daughter's complaints (*Klagen*) by using quotations (sentences) from the Bible like "A time for every purpose under heaven." (*Es gibt für alles eine Zeit.*) Makes all the clothes for her daughter. Cooks "plain food" (*"Hausmannskost"*) according to weekly plans. She calls other kids "heathens" (*Heiden*).

Mr Dewhurst
Likes plain food (*"Hausmannskost"*) like lamb cutlets (*Lammkoteletts*) with green beans and mashed potatoes the best. Doesn't like popular food like pizza or fish and chips. Hates things that can be bought in shops.

"Abomination"
is something living in the cellar that has to be fed (given food) by Martha every day.

(cf. GLATZLE ET AL. 2006: Material p. 3)

One-person presentations
Recitals

Other forms of speaking that are hardly practiced in today's communicative classroom are speeches and recitals. Why not have readers give speeches from the point of view of one (favorite or least favorite) character or write a speech addressed to a character and then give the speech in class? Why not recite passages that readers think are especially well written or typical for the characters. In verse novels like *Out of the Dust* and *by the river*, the original poetry and/or readers' imitation of the original may be recited. While speeches are given and passages are recited, the rest of the class listens, with or without the help of observation tasks.

Recitals and speeches: only one person speaks – the class listens

Chapter 3 Young adult fiction for foreign language development

Expert presentations in exhibitions

Look, think first; then listen

In presentations, usually one person or a small group has prepared a presentation for the whole class. In this currently frequently used form, single students are supposed to speak loud and freely in front of the class. Often, visual aids in the form of posters, pictures, and power point presentations are used. It is usually hard for listeners to just listen. Therefore, all presentations should first be displayed in an exhibition form and students walk through the "gallery". Later, individual presentations which seemed especially interesting to a majority of students can be held.

Two-minute presentations

Limit the presentation to two minutes

Every student should have prepared his/her presentation. A name card is drawn from a box. This student has to present the most important part in no more than two minutes. Listeners take notes like this:

What I have learned:
What remains unclear:
What I have to ask:
These notes are compared with a partner before the presenter is asked (see chapter 6).

> **TIP**
>
> As a post-reading activity, speaking can take place in simulations too. One such simulation could be a talk show in which guest speakers are asked their opinion on certain controversial issues. Intermediate learners carefully prepare guest speakers' role cards to be able to react spontaneously in the talk shows. The class members who have no roles can act as listeners and observers.
> Examples can be found in Hesse & Putjenter (2000: 33). There students discuss teenage pregnancy following the reading of "Dear Nobody". In a similar manner the necessity of boot camps is discussed after the reading of "Holes" (cf. Bögel & Hesse 2005b: 58).

4 Writing

Writing as a vital communicative activity

No reading classroom without writing! Much has been written about the lack of writing skills and the need for more writing practice at German schools since the communicative turnaround ("*kommunikative Wende*") in the 1970s. At that time, the skill of writing was seen as a selective tool and the importance of oral communication was emphasized. This was based on the fact that oral communication covers the biggest part of everyday communication and everyday communication was what learners were supposed to learn. This is true, but the role of writing as another basic communicative tool and essential learner's skill – ranging from note-taking to creative writing – was overlooked. Today, with the advance of computer technology in everyday situations, more writing is probably being done than ever before, for example in email and text message (SMS) form.

3 Improving "receptive" and "productive" skills

In school contexts, writing has long since acquired new importance, although often under the misused term: "creative writing" (cf. TEICHMANN 1998). "Creative writing", a term adopted from English and American school and university contexts, clearly means writing literature, prose, poetry, and drama. It can be assumed that it entered the German EFL teaching terminology only to turn the rather plain and often hated practice of "writing" into an attractive activity.

Misleading use of the term "creative writing"

Writing's lacking attraction in the EFL classroom has probably led to some negligence in the foreign language teaching field in Germany. WERLICH's text type approach (1988) was a systematic approach mainly for the *Oberstufe* and can hardly be used for the communicative reading classroom for intermediate grades. ASTON's *Text Production* (1994), however, is a very usable workbook for practicing different kinds of writing for different purposes. BLUDAU (1999), to my knowledge, was the first to systematically categorize the writing activities for intermediate learners, in this case for grades five and six. Only recently did KIEWEG (2008) focus on process-oriented writing and provide worksheets for younger learners. He offers a good overview of writing activities and tasks. He states that writing has, until now, been used mainly to copy texts from the blackboard or to copy vocabulary (2009: 2). I hope this is no longer true for German schools. I cannot imagine better writing opportunities than writing on the basis of what a learner has read in a book, seen in a film, or experienced himself/herself.

The lacking attraction of writing

In *Jugendliteratur als Schreiblehre* (HESSE 2002a: 135ff.) and in the teacher's handbook for Sachar's *Holes* (BÖGEL & HESSE 2005b), a great variety of writing tasks were applied to the intermediate (late *Mittelstufe*) reading classroom. *Torn Away* by the Canadian author JAMES HENEGHAN and *Holes* by the American LOUIS SACHAR were used as a basis on which communicative, systematic, and meaningful writing was to be taught and learned. Writing firstly means writing about the novel learners have read. Writing in this context is a tool for readers to make sense of what they are reading: they take notes, organize their thoughts, and visualize texts; in other words, they write to grasp the text thoroughly and to respond to it in a receptive and a productive way.

Systematic writing on the basis of motivating novels and meaningful tasks

Oftentimes writing has to be used to prepare oral communication, because writing makes readers think before they speak, a necessity that is often overlooked in the German oral-dominated EFL classroom.

Preparatory writing

But writing itself, of course, is also communication with others and can be used as such in class contexts among readers. Notes, emails, and letters can be exchanged with individuals, but the class as a whole can also create a "wallpaper" that is spread out on the classroom floor where learners can give their written responses to each other while speaking is

Communicative writing

forbidden (cf. GLATZLE ET AL. 2005). It is self-evident that letters can also be addressed to authors, other readers, and journalists and that posters can be used for exposition purposes and for websites as a way to communicate with other classes etc.

Writing based on the novel *Holes*

Holes – a short summary

Holes, the bestselling novel and 1999 winner of the Newbery Medal, tells the story of Stanley Yelnats who is wrongly sentenced to 18 months in an isolated Texan boot camp for juvenile delinquents. He is charged with having stolen the valuable sneakers of the famous baseball star Clyde Livingston, but in fact he was accidentally hit by the shoes as they fell from a bridge.

When Stanley arrives at Camp Green Lake, he sees that there is no lake, only a desert-like landscape in which the boys have to dig a five-foot-wide and five-foot-deep hole every day, supposedly a character building measure. Soon Stanley realizes that the camp's female warden is really using the boys to look for something valuable, the hidden treasure of Kissin' Kate Barlow, a famous Western outlaw.

In the camp, Stanley makes friends with Hector Zeroni, who is called Zero. Their friendship intensifies when they flee from the camp. With a little bit of luck and the help of their own newly acquired skills, they survive in the desert and on sneaking back to the camp, they really find the treasure that the warden has been looking for all her life. Their luck becomes complete when Stanley's parents, who had been too poor to afford a lawyer earlier, employ one who frees both Stanley and Zero from the camp and takes them home.

Holes, a book suitable for a wide range of writing tasks

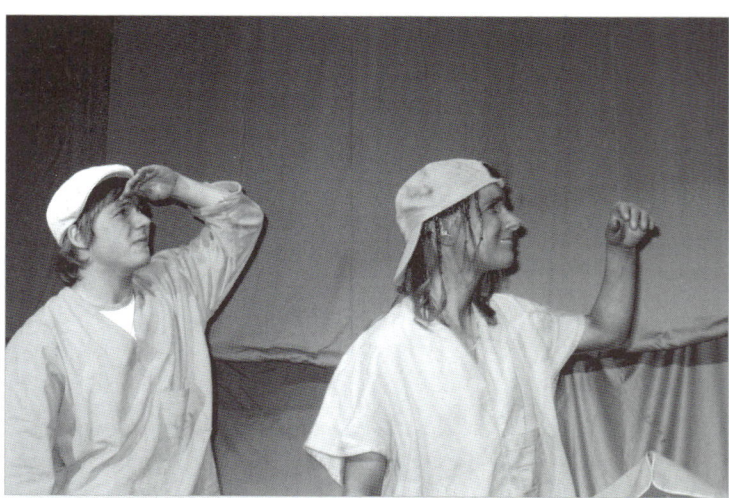

Stanley (Thomas Schiffers) and Zero (Meike Lang) looking for "God's Thumb" in the play *Holes* (PH Freiburg 2005)

3 Improving "receptive" and "productive" skills

The novel is a family story, a problem story, an adventure story, a fairy tale, and a humorous story accompanied by a good Hollywood film with the same title (2003). As such, it is highly recommended for grades 9 and 10 (cf. BÖGEL & HESSE 2005a). With guided help all kinds of writing can be practiced so that students are systematically prepared for the writing that they are generally graded on, but for which they are seldom given badly needed support (cf. BÖGEL & HESSE 2005b).

The following table gives an overview of all the systematic writing that can be learned when dealing with SACHAR's *Holes*, including many communicative text types. It is meant as a way to combine the reading of a motivating novel with systematic writing activities to prepare students for writing in advanced classes (*Oberstufe*) later on. It was also meant as a counter argument to the prevalent teachers' statement that there is too little time to read novels in intermediate grades (*Mittelstufe*).

Learning to write systematically

The table below lists all text types (printed in bold type) based on *Holes*. As one can see in the table, the term "creative writing" is also used, but only for creative "gap filling" activities in which students can write their own stories or endings and fill gaps in the text that authors leave for readers to respond to their texts. The letter W stands for "Worksheet").

Forms of writing tasks and text types

Preparatory writing	Personal writing	Expository writing	Creative writing
Note-taking: Stanley's Profile (W 1) Crossword Puzzle (W2) Family tree (W 5) The beginning of a friendship: Stanley and Zero (W 8) Description of the camp (W 4) and the guards (W 12) Film: Bootcamp (W 20) **Connecting sentences:** Kate Barlow's Story (W 10) **Filling in forms:** Stanley's crime (W5) character files (W 6) Wanted poster (W 11)	**Personal letter:** letter to Stanley's mother (W 9) **Formal letter:** letter to the Attorney General (W 13) **Report:** steps to friendship (W 18)	**Summary:** film and book review (W 21) **Narration:** Stanley's crime (W 5) **Historical narration:** Kate Barlow (W 10) **Analytical description:** steps to friendship (W 18) **Description of the camp** (W 4) **Characterization:** character files (W 6) character relationships (W 7) **Comparison and contrast:** film and reality (W 19) **Formal letter:** letter to the Attorney General (W 13)	**Story** of Stanley's crime (W 3) **Interior monologue:** Stanley's new sense of self (W 15) **Poem/song:** "If only" (W 19) **Advertisement:** Camp Green Lake (W 14) **TV script** for a Sploosh commercial (W 17) **Interview** with Stanley's father (W 16) Wanted **poster** (W 11)

Chapter 3 Young adult fiction for foreign language development

Preparatory writing	Personal writing	Expository writing	Creative writing
Advertisement: Camp Green Lake (W 14) Sploosh commercial (W 17)		**Argumentation:** panel discussion (W 21) **Comparison and contrast essay:** the guards (W 20)	

(BÖGEL & HESSE 2005b: 7)

Learning to write certain text types, step by step

The following example of a single writing task shows how students are led from note-taking to finally write a vivid story of Stanley's "crime". In step 1, two chapters of the text have to be scanned to find the necessary information to be filled into the table. In step 2a, information concerning the text type is given, accompanied by vocabulary, some of which should be applied to enlarge the vocabulary range; in step 2b, guidelines concerning content and organization of the story are given (cf. BÖGEL & HESSE 2005b). These principles of guiding learners to be able to fulfill the task and to later compare their writing to the model text also make it possible to use the workbook for independent study purposes.

Learning to rewrite a story

Sample task: Re-writing a story – Stanley's crime
Stanley had to go to court. The judge sent him to Camp Green Lake. Enter his data into the file that is sent to the camp. (chapters 3 and 6)

Note taking before writing a continuous text

Step 1: Stanley's criminal record

Profile sheet for	Stanley Yelnats
Name	Stanley Yelnats
Age	13?
Place of residence	California
Crime	Stole a pair of shoes from display at the homeless shelter which famous baseball player Clyde Livingston had donated to the shelter. Auction and autograph signing would have brought in at least 5,000 dollars.
Criminal record	first criminal offense
Sentence	18 months of detention
Sent to	Camp Green Lake, Texas

Thinking about form and style

Step 2: Write Stanley's version of his crime.
a. How a story is told
▶ Write it as vividly as you can
▶ Use details, adjectives, and verbs that add color to your story
▶ Use direct speech

100

▶ You may even use slang (remember you are writing as Stanley who may be mad about a few things)

For this, the following words may come in handy:
to make fun of s.o. – to bully s.o. – bully (n.) – to torment – to curse –
bad, worse, worst –
ratio – notebook – to retrieve – to dump – toilet bowl
freeway overpass – stinking shoes – to hit – right on the head – a case of bad foot odor
to drop
incident – sign of God – destiny – bad luck – to believe in fate –
ancestor – to run in the family
to blame – patrol car – to arrest – to handcuff s.o. – to question s.o.
to donate – homeless shelter – to sign autographs – to raise money

Using vocabulary help given by teachers

b. What has to be told
Tell the story of
▶ how he was made fun of at school
▶ what he experienced on the way home
▶ his encounter with the police

and don't forget to add his views on
▶ his family's bad luck
▶ his being in the wrong place at the wrong time
▶ his great-great grandfather

Think about content and using the support given by the teachers

Model answer (with given vocabulary in bold type):
That day Mrs. Bell had **made fun of** me for the umpteenth time. She used me, the heaviest kid in class, to teach us **ratios**, saying I weighed three times as much as another kid. The **worst thing** is she doesn't even realize what she's doing. And then the bully Derrick **tormented** me again, although he is really much smaller than I am. He stole my **notebook** and when I tried to **retrieve** it, he dumped it in the **toilet bowl** in the boys' bathroom. By the time I fished it out of the bowl, the bus had gone so I had to walk home. **Exactly while** I was thinking about having to copy the wet pages and **cursing** Derrick, exactly when I was walking under the bridge of the freeway overpass, these stinking shoes fell from the sky and hit me right on the head. Somebody must have really had **a bad case of foot odor** here!
Anyway, I saw this **incident** as **a sign from** God and of **destiny** – all my family **believes in fate** and most of it **we blame on** my no-good-dirty-rotten-pig-stealing-great-great-grandfather. I took the shoes with me.
I was running home quickly to give the shoes to my dad, who is trying to discover a way of recycling old sneakers, when **a patrol car** stopped next to me and I was **arrested**. I was handcuffed and put into the police car for **questioning**. I didn't understand a thing of what they were talking

Model answer to compare and assess student writing

Chapter 3 Young adult fiction for foreign language development

about and the police took a long time to tell me their story: the shoes had not **dropped from** the sky, but were the shoes of the famous **baseball star** Clyde Livingston. He had **donated** them to our local **homeless shelter**, which was going to invite famous people to have the "homeless dinner", with Clyde being there to **sign autographs**. The sneakers were to be auctioned and the organizers expected **to raise** at least five or six thousand bucks. Once again I was in the wrong place at the wrong time like many of my ancestors had been. It was just another example of **bad luck** that seems **to be running in the family** (BÖGEL & HESSE 2005b: 11).

Visualization of a text

As readers constantly have to visualize what they are reading, teaching writing in EFL classrooms should also help practice visualization: drawing graphs, designing models, creating advertisements (for a book, the camp etc.), designing new covers, writing captions or speech bubbles for a picture story or a comic, writing headlines etc. are motivating tasks for readers.

The reading journal

The reading journal as a mirror of an individual response to a text

One popular task among reading teachers is the reading journal (also called reading log, reading diary etc.), which is one way of putting the reader response theory into practice. Readers can write their own responses to what they are reading, can collect questions, statements, personally meaningful text excerpts, write letters to protagonists, rewrite prose as poetry, write (parts of) the story from a different point of view, visualize what they are reading in drawings etc. The reading journal is often very interesting to read if it mirrors conscientious readers' responses. For some learners, it is also a welcome way of being able to actively do something, one reason being to better their grades. Here is an information sheet to distribute in class:

> Buy yourself an extra nice notebook. You may:
> ▶ write very personal responses to certain parts: spontaneous reactions, questions, predictions (ideas on how the book might go on) …
> ▶ add materials by using newspapers, magazines, encyclopedias, internet and other sources to find out more about similar literature, the author, her works …
> ▶ write the journal as a diary from one person's point of view (use hints from the text and your own imagination)
> ▶ add vocabulary that is interesting, typical, necessary to describe certain facts, events, characters …
> ▶ order this vocabulary in a mid map or categorize it
> ▶ make dialogues from narrated parts
> ▶ write a script for a play or a film
> ▶ collect the vocabulary in word fields (you may team up with a partner who specializes in another word field and later put everything together)

3 Improving "receptive" and "productive" skills

> - collect additional texts
> - select music that might match the atmosphere
> - make a list of film titles that deal with the same or with a similar topic
> - find poetry that fits
> - write your own poetry
> - rewrite parts that you don't like (beginning, ending …)
> - draw pictures or find paintings, photos that might fit
> - design your own book cover
> - write a book review for other students at www.amazon.de
> (cf. HESSE 1999: 30)

It has to be noted, however, that some students – often males – do not like to keep reading journals. If teachers make it compulsory, or if keeping the journal is not part of the unit plan (according to which they would be allowed to write in class), they will find that these readers may have written a few sloppy pages shortly before the hand-in deadline. Therefore students who dislike the task should be given a selection of other tasks. Smith and Wilhelm (2002) have pointed out that many male students do not like reflecting too much on characters, problems etc. and prefer to follow the hands-on, practical approach.

Equivalent tasks for males and other reluctant journal writers!

A selection of tasks for these particular students, using *Holes* as an example, could be:
- Draw the landscape described in the novel
- Build a set for the play *Holes*
- Build an architecture model of the camp
- Make a web quest for *Holes*
- Make a website for *Holes* with a variety of tasks and texts, to which international students (the book is read in the whole world) are asked to respond
- Research other novels for teenagers with similar topics and explain the differences and similarities to the class
- Research real life boot camps in the USA and in Germany Explain the different styles
- Film scenes from the book that you have acted out or record a radio play with appropriate sounds and music
- Write English subtitles for the German film *Das Geheimnis von Green Lake*

Alternatives to reading journals

> **TIP**
>
> *The teacher's guide to Holes makes it possible for students to work on their own since every step for every text type is explained. Reflect whether it may be a good idea to have students read and write about the book individually. Think of single students and classes for whom this might be appropriate.*

4 Suggestions for literary projects

1 Identification, empathy and change of perspective in acting

Change of perspective through acting

As stated repeatedly in previous chapters, one of the main goals of reading YA fiction is to be confronted with young protagonists' lives, to feel with them, to compare their lives to readers' own lives, to empathize with them. Changing perspectives helps learners to do just this. Therefore I cannot imagine a better way of changing perspectives than acting out scenes since it involves the whole personality of a learner. "Playing" scenes (as the word says) does not only give insight into protagonists' lives but also provides the classroom with a "playful" atmosphere (cf. NÜNNING & SURKAMP 2006: 142ff.). "Playacting" in the realm of fiction can be done in various forms: in reading in roles, in role plays as lead-ins (as explained in the previous chapter) or at various stages in the reading process, in playing selected scenes, or in dramatizing a whole work of fiction. In the following example I will present a high school project, in which *The Giver* was dramatized by a 10th grade Gymnasium class at the Philipp-Reis-Schule Friedrichsdorf (PRS), an additive comprehensive school.

First example: *The Giver* at high school

Literary projects for project weeks and project exams

In recent years, more and more projects are done in schools on project days, in project weeks, for project exams etc. Students at *Haupt-* and *Realschulen* in Baden Württemberg and in other German *Bundesländer* have to give presentations as part of final exams. Would it not be possible for them to act out scenes, film them, and present them to the public and their examiners?

Acting projects

In project weeks, class contributions for competitions like *Bundeswettbewerb Fremdsprachen* can be prepared, which is usually motivating for classes who want to apply their learned skills in larger contexts and not only show their knowledge to teachers within the confined space of tests! Projects are a lot of work for all participants, but they are also rewarding, even if one does not win a prize. It is self-evident that through constant language training basic skills are also improved.

In the case of teaching in a 10th grade class at PRSF in 1999, a combination of reading and acting out *The Giver* was intended from the very beginning. As is often the case, these 10th graders were bored after five years of textbook work and asked for projects involving motivating literature. After dealing with *Torn Away* in a variety of creative forms in grade 9 (HESSE 2002a), the class chose to read and play *The Giver* in the following year.

The project involved the following: reading the whole novel rather quickly, deciding on three acts with exposition, climactic plot points and denouement according to FIELD (1984), writing a script, and finding ac-

1 Identification, empathy and change of perspective in acting

tors/actresses and the supporting team. All of this was done by dividing up the tasks so that every one of the 28 students had a task he/she was responsible for. In class everybody was introduced to scriptwriting, since this is a basic writing skill in an acting- and action-oriented classroom (cf. WILHELM 2002).

As the teacher, I had dramatized chapter 5 of the novel as a model (HESSE 1999: 34ff.), which was then acted out by various groups. The chapter, showing the community's way of dealing with Jonas' emerging sexuality, is especially motivating for adolescent students. Being much shorter than the chapter itself, the play version just focuses on Jonas' dream, which is crucial for Jonas' development: he later stops taking the pills altogether, a further step in his increasingly critical attitude towards the society.

Learning to dramatize prose

Chapter 5: Jonas' First Stirrings
The Family's Dream Telling Ritual in the Morning

Characters: Mother, Father, Jonas, Lily

The family is sitting at the breakfast table

Mother
   Jonas, it's your turn.

Jonas *(shifting in his chair)*
   I did dream last night.

Father
   Good, Jonas, tell us.

Jonas
   The details aren't clear really, I think I was in the bathing room at the House of the Old.

Father
   That's you were yesterday.

Jonas *(nodding)*
   But, it wasn't really the same. There was a tub, in the dream. But only one. And a real bathing room has rows and rows of them. But the room in the dream was warm and damp. And I had taken off my tunic, but hadn't put on the smock, so my chest was bare. I was perspiring because it was so warm. And Fiona was there, the way she was yesterday.

Mother
Asher too?

Jonas *(shaking his head)*
It was only me and Fiona, alone in the room standing beside the tub. She was laughing, but I wasn't. I was almost a little angry at her, in the dream because she wasn't taking me seriously.

Lily
Seriously? About what?

Jonas *(uneasy)*
I think I was trying to convince her that she should get into the tub of water. I wanted her to take off her clothes and get into the tub of water. I wanted to bathe her. I had the sponge in my hand. But she wouldn't. She was laughing and kept saying 'no'. *(Looking at his parents.)* That's all.

Father
Can you describe the strongest feeling in your dream, son?

Jonas
The wanting. I knew that she wouldn't. And I think I knew that she shouldn't. But I wanted it so terribly. I could feel the wanting all through me.

Mother *(uneasy)*
Thank you for your dream, Jonas.

Father *(getting up from his chair, Lily after him)*
Lily, it's time to leave for school. Would you walk beside me this morning and keep an eye on the newchild's basket? We want to be certain he doesn't wiggle himself loose.
Jonas still in thought rises as well.

Mother
Jonas, wait. I'll write an apology to your instructor so that you'll not have to speak one for being late.

Jonas sinks back down into his chair, watching his mother tidying the remains of the morning meal.
Then she sits down next to him.

1 Identification, empathy and change of perspective in acting

Mother
Jonas, the feeling you described as the wanting?
It was your first Stirrings. Father and I have been expecting
it to happen to you for a long time. It happens to everyone.
It happened to father when he was your age. And it happened
to me. It will happen someday to Lily. And very often, it begins
with a dream.

Jonas
Do I have to report it?

Mother
You did, in the dream-telling. That's enough.

Speaker (Chorus)
Treatment must take place. Treatment must take place.
One pill a day against each stirring. One pill against each
stirring. Treatment must take place. treatment ...

Jonas
But what about the treatment? The speaker says the treatment
must take place.

Mother
No, no. It's just the pills. You're ready for the pills. That's all.
That's the treatment for the stirrings. *She goes and gets the pills.*
Here you are Jonas. But don't forget. From now on you have
to take them regularly. One every day, every day of your life
until you get to the House of the Old. All of your adult life.
But it becomes routine, after a while you won't even pay
much attention to it.

Tao Nguyen as Jonas telling about his first "stirrings"
(PRSF 1999)

Chapter 4 Suggestions for literary projects

Imitating the model text

Students were encouraged to use this model text and the following one dealing with "the ceremony of twelve" (Hesse 1999: 34f.) to dramatize other important passages of the novel. Before doing so, the dramatic tension was dealt with in three acts (cf. Field 1984: 128), which resulted in the following diagram:

Finding the most dramatic parts

Act I: Setup: The community is introduced		Act II: Confrontation: Jonas learns about the memories he has to carry for the whole community		Act III: Resolution: Jonas escapes (and reaches "Elsewhere")
	Plot point I Jonas receives his assignment as Receiver of Memories and Giver		Plot point II Jonas witnesses the release of the twin and plans his escape	

(cf. Hesse 1999: 34)

In the PRS acting project the following list was filled in with students' names after the importance and the responsibility of each role had been discussed in class. A group of female students volunteered as scriptwriters and later became the film directors as well. Filming and cutting the film proved an extra difficult task, which was found out at the end.

Tasks and roles for the participants

Roles
Stage set, props, mask

Tasks
Scan the text again for information on:

Houses
What are houses like? Furniture, cutlery, crockery…? Find objects that can be used for the play. Design the stage set on paper.

Clothes
What did people wear? Kids, grown-ups, women, men, school teachers, Elders, The Giver? Find clothes for actors/actresses.

Faces:
What are the faces like? Find makeup, design hairstyles … for all characters.

1 Identification, empathy and change of perspective in acting

Script, directing	Write the script for your part in vivid dialogues and stage directions Think about images that show the atmosphere, that can be used on stage. Think of dominant colors, shades?
Acting Jonas Asher Lilly Father Mother The Giver Chief Elder Fiona	Take notes on how the characters appear and behave. Do they develop? How? Why/why not? Describe your character's behavior/development and write it down: Which is the most dramatic part your character is involved in? Describe the relationship you have to the other characters. Imagine what you might be wearing.
Camera, sound, light, cut	What kinds of sounds have to be used to create the specific atmosphere? Find songs that match different scenes. Get information on how the sound/light system works and try it out. Find the necessary equipment. Practice filming and sound recording. Together with the directors, make a plan for how to film.

The final product was a film that competed in the *Bundeswettbewerb Fremdspachen*. It showed scenes filmed on stage and scenes filmed outside. The film did not win an award, but students had worked hard to make the project work. Before, a similar contribution with *The 12th Day of July*, which had been much less challenging, had won a prize. All projects resulted in a motivational boost for most. It must be admitted that for a few, it was too much work and they would have preferred to stay hidden in the classroom. But once the class had decided to participate, there was considerate social pressure on everybody, something that seems to be lacking in the ordinary classroom. The final reward for the *The Giver* production was an appearance on Hessen 3 television on May 20th 1999 in the program "Horizonte", whose hosts praised the students for their outstanding commitment. A discussion between the class and the author, who happened to be in the Frankfurt area at the time, was also shown in the TV program.

Competing with other classes

Second example: *The Giver* at the University of Education
In 2005, *The Giver* was also performed by future teachers studying at the University of Education (Pädagogische Hochschule = PH) in Freiburg, Germany.
The concept is based on cooperative learning (McCafferty et al. 2006), experiential learning (Dewey 1997), and project principles (cf. Legutke 2003; Legutke & Schmidt 2009). All these principles, based on different theories, have the following in common: learning occurs in processes, in

Cooperation and experience in project work

which responsible, individual learners communicate and cooperate according to a negotiated plan, which is constantly revised, if necessary. The process and the product lead to experiences that learners can transfer to other situations. For example, "experiential learning" in this respect predicts that future teachers who take part in such projects will be much better prepared to initiate acting in foreign language contexts with their own students in the future. They know the process and the product and will be able to move from being responsible participants to being responsible teachers. They will have learned to be flexible and competent in unexpected situations (cf. LEGUTKE 2003: 262).

Not only in the teaching literature is acting named the ideal form for changing perspectives, but this is also participants' experience. Two actors stated in their written project reports about their roles in *(Un)arranged Marriage* (see chapter 2.4): *"We both had to play roles which are very different from our ideas for ourselves as being independent, self-reliant, reflective humans. But we had to slip into the shoes of submissive Jas and controlling Daddy-ji and had to understand why they behaved the way they did."* (MERTENS & ROMBACH: Project report for *(Un)arranged Marriage* 2009).

Changing role profiles

The two students also agreed that the profiles they had to write at the beginning about the way they interpreted their own characters were constantly changed throughout the rehearsing process. Directors, assistants, and actors cooperated to find the appropriate representation on stage. Due to the rather small number of actors and actresses, they were not only responsible for learning their roles and acting on stage, but they were also in charge of selecting their own costumes so that special prop and costume designers were not needed.

Interaction between amateurs and professionals

Since universities are much better funded than my former high school was, a professional director, Freiburg freelancer Susanne Franz, could be hired to direct the play. (There are individual cases of schools, however, who also hire professionals for school productions.) The director joins students' ideas with her very own images of the play on stage. She showed us that elaborate costumes and exquisite set design are not important for this kind of theater: For example, the only props for *The Giver* production were a gray table and a gray bench and the only costumes consisted of gray, hooded sweatshirts and gray pants. This lack of color stands for the boring, colorless, inhumane society in which "sameness" rules and every sign of individuality is discarded. Small signs can very well create a big effect! Props, costumes, and make-up, which young players often want for realistic representation, can be reduced to a minimum.

The Giver at PH Freiburg 2005 (v.l.n.r. Father: Melanie Amaya; Lilly: Meike Lang; Jonas: Viktoria Brebic; Mother: Ilona Decker)

2 Learning through watching, listening and responding

Dramatizing a novel and acting it out on stage is not only done for university students' sake. It is also done for high school learners of English. The idea is that the future teachers at the University of Education perform in order to give high school students the opportunity to

- enjoy a morning of listening to the foreign language while watching an exciting play
- try out their English competences (comprehension through listening and watching)
- give them ideas for interesting, challenging, YA novels and plays to be read and possibly acted out in their EFL classrooms
- initiate ideas and trigger interest in performing English plays at their own schools. (Scripts, props, and costumes can be rented, films can be bought, and professional help can be given.)

University – high school cooperation

No one in the high school student audience should come unprepared to the performances, since a certain amount of previous knowledge is necessary to aid comprehension. Teachers are invited to a preparatory seminar at the local, cooperating Carl-Schurz-Haus, where they are introduced to the play by an overview of the novel the play is based on, an array of different activities that they can use in their classrooms as student preparation, and an introduction to the directing concept. Teachers who do not come to the in-service seminar are sent the materials via email through the local school authorities (*Oberschulamt*). Thus all teachers from all school forms in Südbaden (*Haupt-, Real-, Berufsschule* and *Gymnasiums*) are invited.

Preparation of teachers

Chapter 4   Suggestions for literary projects

Preparation of high school students

The teaching materials sent to the schools are designed for a two-lesson introduction to the class. They usually consist of a few typical scenes from the play's script. During the actual performance, one can sometimes hear young viewers recite the passages as they watch the play. Young learners are also given vocabulary support and while-viewing sheets.

Discussions and feedback after the performance

After the show, some students stay in the performing arts center to ask questions and to give actors and actresses feedback. Some also send feedback in the mail.
The feedback sheets for *(Un)arranged Marriage* (for content of the novel and play see chapter 5) were distributed in English and German:

Examples of two post-viewing feedback sheets

Thinking about the play

Feedback for advanced students

- How did you like the play? What did you like/dislike about it?
- Who was your favorite character in the play? Why?
- What was your initial image of a Punjabi/Indian family before you saw the play or read the book? What kind of image of a Punjabi/Indian family do you have now? Did your image change? If so, how did it change?
- Did the play spark interest in you for the Punjabi or Indian culture?
- Did the play encourage you to question some of your ideas about your own culture? If yes, in how far?
- What do you think are the main differences between Punjabi and Western family life/culture according to the play?
- Do you have any understanding for Daddy-ji? Why do you think Daddy-ji is the way he is?
- Do you have any understanding for Mummy-ji or Harry? Why do you think they are the way they are?
- Would you have behaved in the same way as Manny: take revenge on his family? What other solutions are imaginable?

Nachdenken über das Stück

Feedback for younger students

- Was fandest du gut an der Aufführung.
- Was fandest du schlecht?
- Mit welcher Figur konntest du am meisten mitfühlen? Warum?
- Kannst du auch die unsympathischeren Figuren wie Mannys Vater verstehen? Wie kommt er zu so einer Haltung? Oder seine Mutter? Oder Harry?
- Kannst du dir vorstellen, was die Rache für seine Familie bedeutete? Findest du die Strafe für sie gerechtfertigt?
- Welche andere Möglichkeit hätte Manny gehabt statt sich an seiner Familie zu rächen?

2 Learning through watching, listening and responding

Even weeks after the performances, teachers sent back students' written responses, from grade 8 to grade 13, all in English:
One 10th grader wrote:

One student's response

I think the students played very well. My favourite actors were Manjit, the main character and his father. I liked that they spoke very clearly and loudly and I liked the music.
The pronunciation was very good! The background was lovely created. I think the actors played well, but the English wasn't always so good.
The end was strange; Why did Manjit think a lot about how to escape from the wedding and then he just left?
The actors were very good, but I would have liked if men had been played by men!
I liked the Indian accent. They imitated it very well.

(Un)arranged Mariage (2008) was part of a series of five Young Adult plays performed once a year by PH students for schools in Südbaden. *Out of the Dust (2004), Holes (2005), The Giver (2006)* and *Give a Boy a Gun (2007)*, had been played previously. Project participants are no acting specialists. The course, that does not require any acting experience, is offered to every student at the PH Freiburg once a year so that about 60 different university students and practicing teachers have acted for more than 5000 high school students so far.

v.l.n.r. (Mother: Stephanie Liebe; Manny: Amelie Krupke; Father: Marian Mertens)

> **TIP**
> *There are also plays written for young adults, for example in the Collins Educational Series "Plays Plus". Using a play written by a professional has many advantages, but dramatizing remains a good task for meaningful classroom writing. Texts with much dialogue are, of course, much easier to dramatize. But putting descriptive parts into dialogue is also a challenging task. Try it out!*

5 Reading with weak, reluctant readers

1 What weak, mostly male, reluctant readers want

Extensive reading with reluctant readers

Many readers will contend that extensive reading classes and reading-turned-into-acting projects are only for university students or, at best, "Advanced Placement" (*Gymnasium*) students, who are supposedly more motivated than other high school students. Admittedly, the high school drama project described in the previous chapter was carried out in a *Gymnasium* class, but meanwhile in Südbaden and Hessen, one mixed-ability class and two *Realschule* classes have played *Holes* for their school communities using the PH model that they had previously seen performed on stage.

Action vs. feelings?

WILHELM (2002: 8ff.) argues that mixed-ability classes with many male "non-readers" are best taught with "action" or "enactment" strategies, a statement that is supported by his own research based in comprehensive American schools. In his previous books (1997; SMITH & WILHELM 2002), he reported how engaged especially at-risk and reluctant learners had become through action strategies. "Enactment" means: "creating situations in which we imagine to learn" (WILHELM 2002: 8). Students are invited to actively imagine, depict characters, forces, or ideas referring to the past, present, and future. Teachers can help students create text interpretations with artistic, aesthetic, and metaphorical meanings. As previously stated, WILHELM's research seems to contradict SAX's statement that strategies which ask students to "feel with the characters" are "girls' tasks" (108). One can only assume that SAX criticizes the overuse of such imaginative tasks, which, he argues, leads to boys' lack of reading interest. He presents map drawing as an alternative for boys – in this case of the *Lord of the Flies* island –, which, I agree, is a good task. But as I suggest in chapter 3.2, it works best if students can choose from a variety of tasks.

My own experiences are similar to WILHELM's: When I taught 9th–10th graders, both male and female students enjoyed the "hands-on" approach to literature, which involves individual tasks (not everyone has to do the same assignment) and different roles (boys do not have to play grandmothers if they don't want to, which SAX criticizes), allows movement in the classroom, and uses young people's creativity.

What boys want

The boys in WILHELM's study expressed a desire for
▶ a challenge that requires skills including assistance to meet challenges, clear goals, and feedback with the chance to make or do something, applying or using what they have learnt,
▶ a sense of control connected with the opportunity to make choices, displaying newly acquired competences,
▶ social activity such as group work on something meaningful
▶ fun and humor (WILHELM 2002: 15).

Action strategies

WILHELM's *Action Strategies for Deepening Comprehension* (2002) is basically a theory-based activity book, an annotated list of action strategies which explains, exemplifies, and specifies all of these strategies teachers can choose from to deal with any piece of literature (45ff.). He applies the strategies to the short story "Fan Club", a story about bullying written by a teenager. Since WILHELM's book is not easily available in Germany, I have provided a (shortened) list. He calls his enactment strategies "reading strategies", which they in fact are, but they are not to be confused with my list in chapter 3.3. WILHELM's definitions reflect that reading strategies do not always have to be trained by filling in worksheets, but can be practiced with activities that require students to be active. These strategies should not only be motivating for so-called "nonreaders" but also for other learners who often complain about the text-centered approach in all subjects (writing and discussing) and the lack of active student participation. The action strategies help students to "recognize, imagine and reconstitute textual meaning, and they reflect and work on it, transforming it and trying it out, along with alternate meanings" (139).

Action strategies to construct meaning

WILHELM's "reading" strategies
Pre-reading
Frontloading: students brainstorm and collect what they already know

Reading comprehension through action

While-reading:
- Role play: students adopt positions of each character
- Flashback drama: students represent a scene displaying what happened before the incident
- Doodling: Students draw a character's inner feelings and present this as a school counselor
- Role play: authority figures are played
- Hot seat/inner voice: students interview and are interviewed in their roles
- Hot seat: a character is interviewed in a press conference
- Postcards from the past: students design a postcard from the past, which might be important to the current situation
- Missing scene drama: Students notice a missing scene and fill this textual gap
- Radio talk show: students respond to story as radio talk show hosts and callers
- Vote with your feet: students show their position on an issue or a dilemma by stamping their feet
- Whispers/good angel: students decide what a character needs to know and say and whisper it to the acting student
- Choral montage of lines: students write a poem from notes between two characters, which can be spoken in a chorus

Chapter 5   Reading with weak, reluctant readers

- Tableau and statue: students create visual pictures with their bodies to emphasize detail, meaning, and relationships
- Scene after the story: students represent a scene that captures consequences

Post-reading
"Mantle of the expert" and talk show: follow-up on issues raised; transfer of literature to real-life situations (41ff.).

2 Reading material for weak, reluctant readers

Light reading!

What was mentioned earlier about motivating reading materials for the general student population is, of course, even truer for reluctant readers. Readers with no or very little reading experience outside school have to be offered easy books, books dealing with popular themes, including non-fiction and how-to books.

Appealing design!

Books have to be short; print has to be large; illustrations have to be easy; annotations must be provided; some should be based on other popular media that many students know. Graphic novels and comics with little text, popular themes, maybe based on other media, are most appealing.

Example of a motivating text for weak learners

One problem with providing interesting, understandable texts for these students is the material that is available on the educational publishing market. A Freiburg *Hauptschule* class I once observed was fascinated with excerpts of Charles Bukowski's *Ham on Wire*. After a small reading unit done on the basis of *Ham on Wire*, they appreciated this kind of literature. They said they liked it because it was different from the material they were usually exposed to.

In the few excerpts they read of this autobiographical account, Bukowski describes the problems he had as an immigrant kid coming to America from Nazi Germany. He had lots of street fights with "real Americans". He skipped school and went to bars with friends instead. He was beaten by his drunken father and was often drunk himself.

First problem: censorship for motivating texts

When a European educational publisher was asked to publish the first-hand account of Bukowski (a rather well-known, but also notorious writer) in an easy reader format, they refused. They claimed that the content of the book, which deals with violence to a large extent, was not appropriate for school.

It is obvious: The educational publishing market is prone to banning the books these types of students might enjoy. That is one problem teachers might face if they want to get these students to read. One way out of this dilemma is for teachers to use excerpts from, shorten, simplify, and annotate appropriate books themselves. The other option is to create a book box with easy, illustrated, popular material.

Second problem: applying materials to learners' needs means extra work for teachers

3 Individual reading: Working with book boxes

In a book box for reluctant readers, materials have to be included that teachers may not even like themselves since they may seem cheap, formulaic, stereotypical, fast-paced, or maybe even violent; in other words, books that are not considered educationally valuable. According to KRASHEN, the most powerful way to encourage children to read is to expose them to "light reading". Light reading is probably the kind of reading educationalists and reading advocates did when they were young (cf. 2004: 92). As light reading, KRASHEN proposes comic books such as the *Archie* series, teen romances, and magazines. He refers to studies showing that light reading has had a great effect on students' reading competence (cf. 111 ff.). NEWKIRK suggests books like the *Captain Underpants* series that boys obviously like for their crazy, "potty" humor.

Third problem: texts learners like are disliked by many teachers

The class book box may contain so-called "chick lit", novels similar to the *Sweet Valley* or *The Babysitter's Club* series for girls. To be able to read in English, I assume weak female readers would not object to *Sweet Valley Kids*, a series that is actually written for much younger readers, before they move on to the *Sweet Valley Twins* and *Sweet Valley High* series, which is more age-appropriate.
KRASHEN reports that Korean adult learners of English became avid readers after they had discovered the easy *Sweet Valley Kids* series (2004: 13). The box may also contain fashion magazines and magazines for young girls (e.g. *Seventeen*), and how-to-repair-a-car books, computer- and sports books, and magazines for boys. It should contain graphic novels of all kinds, not only the previously recommended ones, but also "cheap" dime novels and magazines. The main idea is that the box is attractive to learners, that they learn the foreign language by reading, and become proud of their own achievement. The more they read, the more competent they will become and will maybe want more challenging books later on.
The good thing about these popular books is that they are often already known from other popular media such as film, TV, or computer games, so learners have some previous knowledge and probably recognize elements of the stories, which help them understand the foreign language texts.
LUMMEL (2008) points out that school staff should cooperate and recommend books to one another, since nobody can keep up with the masses of new publications. Also, the class-library selection of German educational publishers may be used although – especially for reluctant readers – too little attention has been paid to these readers so far.

Texts need not always be not age-appropriate

Chapter 5 Reading with weak, reluctant readers

Class library for reluctant readers

> **CRITERIA**
>
> **... for creating a class library for reluctant readers**
> ▶ The texts should be easy, the vocabulary and grammar basic.
> ▶ The books must be very slim. Good, longer material can be shortened by teachers, student teachers, or future teachers, maybe in installments.
> ▶ Readers must be able to relate to the topic and the style
> ▶ Make sure that interest is aroused based on their previous knowledge.
> ▶ Make sure that stories are exciting, suspenseful, thrilling, scary, and entertaining.
> ▶ Funny, humorous texts are a necessity, even grossly funny books (cf. NEWKIRK 2002).
> ▶ Add non-fiction on how things work, science and technology, and how-to books and magazines.
> ▶ Include material that students already know in German, from books (Die drei ???, Fünf Freunde), from film and TV and computer games. Maybe even German editions can be added?
> ▶ Try out bilingual books! There are some such mystery books on the market.
> ▶ If other media (audio or film versions) are available, let students listen to or watch them with head phones.
> ▶ Start with one book or magazine for every student in class.

4 Funding book boxes

No institutional funding, no books?

To respond to many readers' complaints about the lack of funds to buy books, one must admit that German schools are generally badly equipped with books. Libraries do not exist in many schools in contrast to American schools, which do not only have large libraries but also library personnel always willing to guide students through the large amount of material.

Using other resources

However, in Germany, much can be done to equip classrooms with book boxes or even establish libraries as well:
▶ School *Fördervereine* are only too willing to support reading motivation, the lack of which has shocked the nation since the PISA study.
▶ Publishing companies can be asked to donate books.
▶ Book fairs (Frankfurt, Basel, Leipzig, Cologne) often give away free books to teachers on the last day of the fair.
▶ Check out international schools in your area. They often sell English books at flea markets. The number of international schools is increasing!
▶ Local libraries are sometimes all too willing to cooperate with schools. Ask them to fund an English children's box that can be rented for a period of time.

- Cooperate with a university.
- Money earned at school performances, parties, celebrations can be used for book purchases.
- Class projects, such as writing book recommendations for other students and publishing them in book or CD form, are action-oriented. Books and CDs can be sold to parents, students, and teachers. The money earned can be used to buy more books (cf. HESSE 2003). These projects are plausible for entire schools, too.
- Buy cheap English books at English charity shops. Britain has thousands. Teachers should always travel with an extra suitcase! (There are a few Oxfam shops selling English books in Germany, too!)
- Why not copy American schools in their art of fund raising: sell chocolates, cakes, sell at flea markets, wash cars, paint classrooms, babysit for a good cause, teach parents English, teach how to create websites, teach how to do role plays and other computer games ...; do everything for money and use it for more and more book purchases; there are no limits to fundraising ideas.

6 Class libraries and beyond

1 The book box at the Realschule Kirchzarten

Reading-writing connection

The following small research project using a newly created book box was carried out in the winter semester of 2008/09 at the Realschule in Kirchzarten. Thirty 9th graders were given a book box of about 120 English books from which they were asked to choose a book to read during a vacation. The book box was funded by the Pädagogische Hochschule Freiburg.

Research questions

The student teachers wanted to know
1. what kinds of books learners would choose and
2. how they would show their understanding in writing (using the above worksheet as a guideline)
3. how they would present their book to the class
4. how the class liked the reading experience
5. and what individual interviewees would say (in German) about their experience

Format of the requested book report

The learners' task was to make a book report on the basis of the following model sheet:

Book review and book presentation
Your name:

Author:
Title:
Year of publication:
Country of origin:
Original/or shortened version:
Number of pages:

Genre/type of book:	The book is an information book, a realistic novel, a fantasy book, myth, fairy tale, a family/school/animal-story, a graphic novel, collection of cartoons ….
Plot/Content:	The book is about … It shows/deals with ……… …………………………..
	The sentence I liked most from the whole book is …………………….. because ….
	The most typical sentence for the whole book is ……………………. because
Characters, their ages and their goals (*Ziel*), problems:	The main character(s) is/ are …
	He/she has … They have a problem, conflict, fight with …
	They are victims, robbers, dealers …
	He/she looks like …

1 The book box at the Realschule Kirchzarten

	The character that I liked best is/was .... because ...
	The character I disliked most is/was
	His/her most typical saying is:
Setting	The story is set in (place) .... in (time)....
Point of view:	The novel is written from ....'s perspective.
Your identification as a reader:	(Therefore) I could identify with ..., feel with, was angry at, was happy when ...
Who should (not) read the book:	I would recommend the book for ...., (but not for ....) because ....It would be a good book to read in classIt would be good for the class library
What is good/not so good about the book:	What I especially liked/didn't like about the book was ....
Overall evaluation:	From 1 (lowest) to 5 (best) stars

The following books were chosen:

Book selection

Information books	Number of pages	Gender: boy (b) girl (g)
Kingdom of Kush	24	b
Breaking the Sound Barrier	24	b
Animals of the Tropical Rain Forests	16	b
Tropical Forests	24	b
Polar Bears	106	g
Dinosaurs	24	g
National Geographic Magazine for kids	–	b
Comets	24	b
Biography		
Salt in His Shoes	29	b
Fantasy/mystery		
Frankenstein Moved in on the Fourth Floor	57	b
Eragon (German) not in book box	–	b
Zorro	64	b
Bridge to Terabithia	144	b
Horror at Remsen High	63	g

Chapter 6   Class libraries and beyond

Genre	Number of pages	Gender: boy (b) girl (g)
Animal fantasy		
Four Mice Deep in the Jungle	128	b
Picture book/comic		
Hit It!	80	b
The Boy Who Wouldn't Go to Bed	30	g
Jackie and the Shadow Snatcher	26	b
Realistic fiction		
Green Mile	92	b
Dream On	92	g
All 4 Love	46	g
A Year Down Yonder	160	g
The Clue at the Zoo	74	g
Damian Drooth Supersleuth	59	g
The Case of the Corner Shop Robbers	55	g
The Outsiders	192	b

Here is one example of the learners' book reviews. The writer read one of the more voluminous books. I chose it because his review underscores what the American reading researchers say (cf. SMITH & WILHELM 2002; NEWKIRK 2002 see chapter 5) about boys' reading preferences:

1 The book box at the Realschule Kirchzarten

> Author: Geronimo Stilton
> Year of publication: March 2004
> Country of origin: New York and London
> Title of the book: *Four Mice Deep in the Jungle* (original version)
>
> **The book is a fantasy book about** animals. It shows mice in "New Mouse City" at start, but then one day the mouse Geronimo Stilton must leave the city, because his sister was stressed about he is afraid of very much things. So his sister decided to put him to a trip with the "Survival School" into the jungle. After many adventures he is only afraid of cats, but the doctor calms him down: "it's a normal thing that mice are afraid of cats".
> **The sentence I liked most** from the whole book is: "Then a pigeon decided to poop on my nose", because this sentence is very funny.
> **The most typical sentence** of the whole book is: "But I'm afraid of…, because Geronimo Stilton says it very often.
> **The main character** is a mouse. He is afraid of: flying, the darkness, spiders, snakes, he is vertigo, and so on.
> **His goal is** to be not afraid of these things. He looks like a clever mouse.
> **The character I liked** best was Dr. Shrinkfur, because he gets money for saying: "It's up to you"! At first the story is **set in New Mouse City** the capital of Mouse Island, but than the story is set in Rattytrap Jungle by the Rio Mosquito. **The novel is written** in you/me's perspective.
> **As reader I was really happy** when Geronimo Stilton finished this "Survival School".
> **I would recommend** the book for six up to eleven old kids in England, but in Germany I would recommend it to three or four years English lessons, because it's very easy to understand. It would be good to read in class.
> **What I especially liked** about the book was the good humour. I think I'll give four stars from five to this book.

Example: one male student's review

The written reviews showed that most students had read and understood their books, but most had obviously not used the table as a guideline for writing, which resulted in a lot of mistakes and errors. Only after a group of six university students had discussed the reviews with each individual, were the corrected versions handed out to be used for the upcoming oral presentations.

Reading-writing connection

Speaking alone in front of the class proved to be another big obstacle. Making sure they were understood was not the main aim for most, who were full of anxiety and wanted to get the task over with as quickly as possible. Only the readers who had wholly enjoyed their books and

Reading-writing-speaking connection

Chapter 6 — Class libraries and beyond

wanted to tell the class more about it made it their goal to really inform the class. Therefore, the best presentations were the ones done by learners who were most interested in the topic (not necessarily the ones with the best marks in English, the teacher said). Two of the students whose reviews and presentations mirrored their clear interest in their books, were later interviewed (in German). This was the result:

Interview questions	Answers (girl)	Answers (boy)
1. Was für ein Buch hast du gelesen? Warum hast du gerade dieses Buch ausgewählt?	A Year Down Yonder Ansprechendes Cover, Beschreibung	Comets
2. Wie war es für dich das Buch zu lesen (langweilig, schwierig, einfach)?	Schwierige Vokabeln	Interesse für Wissenschaft und Weltall Sprache einfach, gut verstanden
3. Hat es dir Spaß gemacht? Warum?	Ja, weil es ein Happy End gab	Ja, weil das Buch nicht so lang war
4. Was hat dir keinen Spaß gemacht? Warum?	Zu altmodisch, spielt in 1937	–
5. Das Buch war ja auf Englisch, wie kamst du mit der Sprache zu Recht?	Ok, viele neue Vokabeln	Gut, keine schwierigen Wörter
6. Was hast du gemacht wenn du Probleme hattest (etwas nicht verstanden hast)? → Lesestrategie	Satz mehrmals durchgelesen, dann Wörterbuch	Vokabeln aus Zusammenhang, dann Wörterbuch
7. Glaubst du, dass englische Bücher generell die Sprache verbessern (oder helfen besser zu werden)? z.B. schnelles Lesen, Vokabeln, Satzstrukturen verstehen, heutige Jugendsprache verstehen…	Ja, nicht immer Lehrer fragen, sondern selbstständig lesen und sich um unbekannte Wörter kümmern	Ja, Ausdruck
8. Denkst du, dass das Buch, das du gelesen hast, dein Englisch verbessert hat? Warum? (z. B. schnelles Lesen, Vokabeln, Satzstrukturen verstehen, heutige Jugendsprache verstehen…)	Ja, Ausdruck und Vokabeln	Ein bisschen, Ausdruck, Vokabeln, man beschäftigt sich mit der Sprache

1 The book box at the Realschule Kirchzarten

Interview questions	Answers (girl)	Answers (boy)
9. Welche Bücher interessieren dich auf Deutsch? Kannst du dir auch vorstellen so ein Buch in Englisch zu lesen?	Teeniebücher Ja	Wissenschaft Ja
10. Auf welche Empfehlung würdest du am meisten hören: Eltern, Mitschüler, Lehrer, Studenten, Zeitschriften, Internet …	Gleichaltrige	Freunde
11. Würdest du gerne ein Buch mit der ganzen Klasse lesen? Was für ein Buch wäre das?	Nein, viele würden es nicht verstehen → dauert zu lange	Ja, aber keine langen Bücher

Reflecting on the project

The project was not only a reading project, but it included writing and speaking as well. Silent voluntary reading has not been tried out so far. The results were astonishing in several respects:
- Students obviously did not mind reading the books and writing the reviews in the vacation.
- 26 out of 30 students sent the reviews on time. They appeared to like the idea of using email for an assignment!
- Reading comprehension and writing about it is obviously a very complex task. Students seem to have been focused on reading, but writing was only an additional ill that had to be done. This explains the large number of mistakes and organizational chaos in the first draft.
- Students took the project very seriously. Even the last four students who did not manage to send the reviews on time, did prepare their presentations well.
- Presentations were a very difficult task, especially if one takes the number of onlookers (6 students and 2 teachers) into account. But everyone did it. The time limit of three minutes was appropriate.

This small project that is to be continued seems to be a first step in the right direction. The book box will have to be adapted to students' interests and abilities. More short, maybe even simplified and annotated books, accompanied by Audio CDs will have to be added. The long books remain only for the students who find the task challenging and for a bilingual student. It seems that this first attempt at establishing individual reading was seen as successful. Silent reading should be made possible, without any book review assignments. Maybe a book mark or a library card with a short evaluation in note form should be the only written task.

Chapter 6 Class libraries and beyond

2 Activities for the entire school to promote reading

Reading activities involving the whole school

According to Lummel's research (2008), promoting reading works best if the whole school is involved. Schools can announce book weeks in which the whole school reads one book and classes communicate or even compete with each other. (Whole communities can read a book as well: In Seattle, USA I once saw a billboard saying "Seattle reads *Holes*"!) Theme-based reading on any topic, e.g. "Exploring the world" or "Teenage life" may stimulate reading, as well as book sharing days.

Cooperative reading

Reading does not even have to be a lonesome, separating activity if reading buddies read, discuss, present, or display the same book. Other reading activists propose reading nights, in which students read and spend the night at school (cf. Pott 2007). There seems to be no limit to reading encouragement ideas!

Ideas to promote reading at school

Computer software for EFL classrooms similar to *Antonin*, the program used in German-speaking primary schools for German books, or something like the Accelerated Reader Program (ARP) used in American schools should be created with book recommendations, tasks, and awards.

Authors' visits

Inviting authors to the school seems to boost reading motivation, too. When Native American high school students met with Native American writer Sherman Alexie, boys who had not been avid readers before, were full of praise after Alexie's visit and the realization that *The Absolutely True Diary of a Part-time Indian* was almost totally based on Alexie's autobiographical data. Now they are eagerly awaiting Alexie's next book (cf. Blasingame 2008). A similar, fictional, yet very plausible story, is told by the protagonist in Sharon Creech's *Love that Dog*, when Walter Dean Myers comes to a primary school. Here again, a young black student is excited about a very accessible author who is funny and behaves just like any other person. School visits of English and American authors in Germany are sometimes arranged by publishers, the local *Amerikahäuser*, or by the British Council.

Contact with authors

One can also contact writers by writing to their German or foreign publishers or agents. Authors such as Lois Lowry, James Heneghan, Berlie Doherty and Robert Swindells, can be contacted through their publishers who usually forward the letters on to them. Teachers must know that children's writers – in contrast to adult authors – often consider it their responsibility to respond to young readers. Contact to authors often leads to an increased interest in their books.

2 Activities for the entire school to promote reading

In the following letter to Robert Swindells, one can see that these two *Realschule* students (grade 9) who read *Abomination* in class, have become interested in reading more of Swindells' works:

An example: letter correspondence with Robert Swindells

July 18, 2007

Dear Mr. Swindells,

R. and I are students in K., we read the book Abomination.
We are happy that we can send you this letter.
We want to know how did you get the idea to write this book?
When writing the book where you able to identify with the characters?
We think that the book is really exciting.
We would be happy when you could recommend another book, because we are interested to read your books in English.

Best wishes, and we hope you will write us back
K. and R.

On August 7, 2007 Robert Swindells responded to the whole class and to some students individually:

Authors' interest in what young readers think

Dear students,

Many thanks for your kind, interesting letters. I'm happy to learn that most of you enjoyed ABOMINATION. It is not a true story, but the idea for it came when I read a true story about a child found living in a coop with chickens in France. She was ten years old, and had been kept with chickens from birth. She couldn't stand upright or speak. She squatted, flapping her elbows and making chicken noises. ...

Here is his response to individual students (names have been changed):
The main difference between a teen book and an adult book, Tim is that usually there is very little sex in teen books. This is not because we writers don't want to put sex in teen books, but because it is mostly forbidden by publishers. Some publishers are becoming more relaxed about it.
No, Nadine, I don't know about Jessica in Austria – was she a hidden child?
No, Nora, I'm not religious. I'm a member of the British Humanist Association.

Peace and love
Robert Swindells

Chapter 6 Class libraries and beyond

> **TIP**
> Try to contact the author of a book that you read in class!
> Letters should have a good form so that authors feel intrigued to answer.
> Content, however, is most important. Have your students give their interpretations, individual questions, and ideas.
> Make sure they don't ask personal questions like "how old are you?"

3 Summary and outlook

Summary

This book was meant to be a guide for future teachers and already practicing teachers who
1. want help for the selection of novels to be read in the classroom,
2. want support for a student-centered active classroom, and
3. want to promote individual reading and reading literacy on a larger scale.

Publishers' catalogs lack authentic literature for younger learners

Ad 1: Publishers' YA catalogs are not enough. Today's teenagers and teachers need more titles. Although much YA literature has been added in the last 20 years to German publishers' catalogs, there is still a big gap concerning authentic literature, especially for lower secondary grades (5–8). For lower grades, simplified readers are most readily offered. Shortened, graded readers do have their value, especially the ones that are based on exciting originals. However, their literary quality is often limited: since it is not easy to abridge original material, many times either important parts are left out, "easier" synonyms and sentences have different meanings, and the accompanying pictures are not really appropriate. In addition, most shortened readers are based on classics in children's literature, which are very far removed from the lives of today's teenagers. Especially with the stories for younger readers, I wanted to point at the current large variety of good, funny, exciting, motivating contemporary texts, often accompanied by pictures and other visuals.

Publishers' catalogs lack authentic literature for reluctant learners

Not only for younger readers, but also for reluctant readers at the secondary level, good, motivating reading material is missing on the German EFL market. With the recommendations for reluctant readers, I have tried to fill part of that gap. It is not easy to find easy material for older, reluctant readers since many of the picture books are either too childish or linguistically too difficult. Popular graphic novels that seem very motivating are often too difficult for non-natives, since they draw upon readers' knowledge of informal English and slang. The books recommended here are only a first step towards better supporting teachers in teaching weaker, often reluctant readers.

3 Summary and outlook

I hope that readers of this book will try out some of the suggested books in their EFL classrooms and that publishers will publish some of them in annotated form, maybe even accompanied by teacher's guides. However, the search for more motivating, authentic reading material for reluctant readers is not yet finished. Teachers and students, too, are asked to go on searching. In contrast to only 10 years ago, today, with the help of the internet, one can research and order materials, or research on the internet and order materials from local, independent book stores. Some excellent internet research sources are:
http://www.carolhurst.com
http://www.acs.ucalgary.ca/~dkbrown/index.html
http://www.scils.rutgers.edu/professionaldevelopment/childlit/Children Lit/index.html

Outlook: Publishers enlarge their *Lektüre* pool; teachers try out and research new materials

Ad 2: The practical part of this book was supposed to give teachers help when dealing with long texts. Problems with extensive reading are tackled not only with motivating material, but with reading strategies, especially for learners who have relatively little reading experience. This should help readers to enjoy reading more!

Enjoyment through more efficient reading

With the emphasis on "action", it is self-evident that both a process and a product approach in an active, learner-centered, task-based classroom is applied. Especially by showing how fiction is turned into drama by learners themselves, I wanted to exemplify how even intermediate learners' linguistic competence and creativity can be used and in how far both can be improved in a high school project.

Learner-centered action and creativity in the classroom

If readers of this book want more concrete help to plan and carry out teaching units with certain books, the frequently mentioned teacher's guides can be consulted, which every educational publisher offers. They demonstrate in detail how a work plan based on a certain novel can be created, how the unit may be broken down into single lessons; they present teaching goals, learner activities for certain parts of the book; they collect and present vocabulary necessary for speaking and writing about the whole book; they remark on the setup of an active, workshop-like classroom. Often additional transfer material is provided for learners to be able to apply what they have learned to other themes and new situations (see chapters 4 and 5). Teachers trying out new materials can also give publishers tips and recommendations and can publish their own teacher's guides.

Concrete tips for teaching novels

Ad 3: We have reason to believe that schools and teachers in supporting students with motivating reading material and focusing more on reading in schools will contribute to an increase in reading motivation and reading literacy. In the USA, where reading has to compete even more than in Europe with other media and with a huge sports culture, reading is on the rise. The 2009 National Endowment for the Arts report documents "a significant turning point in recent American cultural history" (http://www.nea.gov/research/ReadingonRise.pdf). Young adults' (18–24) reading rates showing the largest declines in earlier surveys, demonstrate a 21-percent growth in 2009. The authors of the report consider the increased high school reading initiatives a crucial contributing factor to this increase: "During their high school years, they were the target of the largest literary initiatives in the agency's history, and we note their progress with particular satisfaction" (1). The 2004 report, based on a 26-year-old questionnaire, had revealed a steady decline (cf. http://www.nea.gov/news/news04/ReadingAtRisk.Html).

Hopeful outlook

The German initiatives – on a national and a local basis – may give hope as well. Stiftung Lesen (http://www.stiftunglesen.de), with its nationwide reading projects and local initiatives, with reading tutors in communities and schools (http://www.wirlesenvor.de), is using similar ideas, although these are still not as numerous and as diverse as the American ones (see also chapter 1).

This book was meant as a step towards supporting EFL reading literacy, which also helps literacy in the native tongue (KRASHEN 2004). We can do much more, as LUMMEL's model at his Bavarian school (2008) and the American example show.

Bibliography

Primary literature

ADAMS, RICHARD: *Watership Down.* London: Scribner 2005

ALEXANDER, LLOYD: *The Chronicles of Prydain.* New York: Dell 1964

ALEXIE, SHERMAN: *The Absolutely True Diary of a Part-Time Indian.* New York: Little Brown & Co. 2007

ALMOND, DAVID: *Skellig.* London: Hodder 1998

ANDERSON, LAURIE HALSE: *Speak.* New York: Puffin 2001

ANDERSON, MATTHEW T.: *Octavian Nothing.* Somerville/MA: Candlewick Press 2006

ANDERSON, MATTHEW T.: *Feed.* Somerville/MA: Candlewick Press 2002

ANONYMOUS: *Arabian Nights.* New York: Norton 2008

APPLEGATE, KATHERINE & ORMEROD, JAN: *The Buffalo Storm.* New York: Clarion Books 2007

ARMSTRONG, JENNIFER & SMITH, JOSEPH: *Audubon: Painter of Birds in the Wild Frontier.* New York: Harry N. Abrams 2003

ARTHUR, ROBERT & HITCHCOCK, ALFRED ET AL.: *Alfred Hitchcock and The Three Investigators.* New York: Random House 1965 –1987

AUGUSTYN, BRIAN & BURCHETT, RICK: *Batman. The Mad Hatter.* New York: Scholastic 2004 (Reader level 3)

AUSTER, PAUL: *Brooklyn Follies.* New York: Picador 2006

BANKS, LINDA REID: *The Indian in the Cupboard Trilogy.* New York: HarperCollins 2004

BAWDEN, NINA: *The Witch's Daughter.* London: Puffin Books 1973

BENETT, ALAN: *The Uncommon Reader.* London: Profile Books 2008

BLACKMAN, MALORIE: *An Eye for an Eye.* London: Corgi Books 2003

BLUME, JUDY: *Then Again, Maybe I Won't.* London: Yearling 1986 [1971]

BLUME, JUDY: *Forever.* New York: Simon & Schuster. Reissue 2007 [1975]

BLYTON, ENID: *Five on a Treasure Island. (Famous Five Series).* London: Hodder Children's Books. New edition 2001

BLYTON, ENID: *Five on a Treasure Island. Easy Readers B.* Aschehoug/Denmark 1942

BLYTON, ENID: *Secret Seven Win Through (Secret Seven Series).* London: Hodder 2006

BOYNE, JOHN: *The Boy in the Striped Pyjamas.* London: Random House 2006

BRIGGS, RAYMOND: *Gentleman Jim.* London: Jonathan Cape 2008

BROWNE, ANTHONY: *Willy the Dreamer.* Cambridge: Candlewick Press 1998

BROWNE, ANTHONY: *Bear Goes to Town.* London: Hamish Hamilton 1982

BROWNE, ANTHONY: *Look what I've Got.* London: Julia MacRae Books 1980

BROWNE, ANTHONY: *My Dad.* New York: Farrar Straus & Giroux 2000

BROWNE, ANTHONY: *My Mum.* London: Random House 2005

BROWNE, ANTHONY's *King Kong. From the story conceived by Edgar Wallace and Merian C. Cooper.* London: Picture Corgi 2005

BRUCHAC, JOHN & MAGNUSON, DIANA: *Trail of Tears.* London: Random House 1999

BRUCHAC, JOHN: *The Winter People.* New York: Puffin 2004

BRUCHAC, JOHN: *Code Talker.* New York: Penguin 2005.

BUSCH WILHELM: *Max und Moritz.* Zürich: Diogenes 1973 [München: Braun u. Schneider 1917]

BULL, JANE: *Make It.* London: Dorling Kindersley, 2008

BUNTING, EVE: *Dandelions.* Port Orchard/WA: Sandpiper 2001

CARD, ORSON SCOTT: *Ender's Game.* New York: Hyperion 2008

CART, MICHAEL (Ed.): *Necessary Noise.* New York: HarperCollins 2003

CART, MICHAEL (Ed.): *Tomorrowland.* New York: Scholastic 1999

Bibliography

CART, MICHAEL (Ed.): *Sex and Love.* New York: Simon & Schuster Children's Publishing 2001

CHAMBERS, AIDAN: *This Is All.* London: Random House 2005

CIENCIN, SCOTT & BURCHETT, RICK: *Batman Green Gotham.* New York: Scholastic 2005 (Reader level 3)

COLE JOANNA & DEGEN, BRUCE: *The Magic School Bus on the Ocean Floor.* New York: Scholastic 1994

COLFER, EOIN: *Artemis Fowl.* New York: Hyperion 2008

COLVILLE, BRUCE & CATHERINE: *Space Brat.* New York: Aladdin 1992

COLVILLE, BRUCE & CATHERINE: *The Dragon of Doom.* New York: Aladdin 2005

COOPER, SUSAN: *King of Shadows.* New York: Simon & Schuster 2001

CORNELISSEN, CORNELIA: *Soft Rain.* New York: Dell 1998

CREECH, SHARON: *Love That Dog.* New York: HarperCollins, 2001

CREW, LINDA: *Children of The River.* New York: Laurel Leaf 1991

CROSS GILLIAN: *The Great Elephant Chase.* Oxford: Oxford University Press 1992

CULHANE, KATE & HAGUE, MICHAEL: *A Ghost Story.* New York: SeaStar Books 2001

CURTIN, JEREMIAH: *Irish Tales of the Faeries and of the Ghost World.* Mineola/NY: Dover 2000

CURTIS, CHRISTOPHER PAUL: *The Watsons Go to Birmingham – 1963.* New York: Laurel Leaf 2000

DAHL, ROALD: *Boy. Tales of Childhood.* London: Puffin Books 1984

DAHL, ROALD: *Going Solo.* London: Puffin Books, 1986

DEAR AMERICA SERIES New York: Scholastic, 1996–2004

DEARY, TERRY & BROWN, MARTIN: *Horrible History Series.* New York: Scholastic 2004–2008

DEFOE, DANIEL: *Robinson Crusoe.* München: Langenscheidt: 2009

DELBANCO, ANDREW (ed.) & DUBOIS, GERARD (Ill.): *Edgar Allan Poe. Stories for Young People.* NewYork: Sterling 2006

DE PAOLA, TOMMY: *Pancakes for Breakfast.* Mooloolaba QLD: Sandpiper 1978

DHAMI, NARINDER: *Bend it like Beckham.* Stuttgart: Klett 2004

DIAKITÉ, BABA WAGUE: *The Hatseller and the Monkeys.* New York: Scholastic 1999

DICAMILLO, KATE: *Tiger Rising.* Sommerville, MA: Candlewick, 2002

DOHERTY, BERLIE: *Dear Nobody.* Stuttgart: Klett 1998

DOHERTY, BERLIE: *Dear Nobody. The Play.* London: CollinsEducational 1995

DOHERTY, BERLIE: *Abela.* London: Anderson 2008

EISNER, WILL: *The Contract with God. Life on Dropsie Avenue.* New York: Norton 2006

DOWD, SIOBHAN: *A Swift Pure Cry.* London: Random House 2006

DOWD, SIOBHAN: *London Eye Mystery.* London: Corgi 2007

ERDRICH, LOUISE: *The Birchbank House.* New York: Hyperion 1999

ESCOTT, JOHN (Ed.): *The Fly and Other Horror Stories.* Oxford: Oxford University Press 2007

FLEISCHMAN, PAUL: *Bull Run.* New York: Harper Collins 1993

FLEISCHMAN, PAUL: *Townsend Warbler.* New York: Harper Collins 1992

FLEISCHMAN, PAUL: *Seedfolks.* Stuttgart: Klett 2001

FLEISCHMAN, SID & SIS, PETER: *The Whipping Boy.* New York: Scholastic 1986

FOREST, ANTONIA: *The Thuggery Affair.* Bath: Girls Gone By 2005

FREEDMAN, RUSSELL: *Lincoln, a Photobiography.* Wilmington: Clarion Books, 1987

FRENCH, FIONA: *Snow White in New York.* Oxford: Oxford University Press 1986

FROST, HELEN: *Keesha's House*. New York: Farrar, Straus & Giroux (FSG) 2003
FROST, HELEN: *The Braid*. New York: FSG 2005
FROST, HELEN: *Diamond Willow*. New York: FSG 2008
GAIMAN, NEIL & MCKEAN, DAVE: *The Day I Swapped My Dad for Two Goldfish*. New York: Harper Collins 2004
GAIMAN, NEIL & MCKEAN, DAVE: *The Wolves in the Walls*. New York: Harper Collins 2003
GAIMAN, NEIL & MCKEAN, DAVE: *Coraline*. New York: Harper Collins 2004
GAIMAN, NEIL & RUSSELL, CRAIG: *Coraline. Graphic Novel*. New York: Harper Collins 2008
GALLO, DONALD R.: *Ultimate Sports. Short Stories by Outstanding Writers for Young Adults*. New York: Bantam Doubleday 1997
GELLETLY, LEEANNE: *Mexican immigration*. Philadelphia: Mason Crest 2004
GEORGE, JEAN CRAIGHEAD: *Julie of the Wolves*. New York: Harper Collins 2003 [1972]
GEORGE, JEAN CRAIGHEAD: *The Witch at Blackbird Pond*. New York: Dell 1993
GEORGE, JEAN CRAIGHEAD: *My Side of the Mountain*. London: Puffin 2000 [1959]
GERSTEIN, MORDICAI: *The Man Who Walked Between the Towers*. Brookfield: Roaring Brook Press 2003
GIFF, PATRICIA REILLY: *A House of Tailors*. London: Yearling 2006
GOETHE, JOHANN WOLFGANG: *Der Zauberlehrling*. Retrieved Mar. 19, 2008 from www.maraba.de/Dichter/goethe4.htm [1798]
GREENE, BETTY: *Summer of My German Soldier*. New York: Laurel Leaf 2006
GÜNDISCH, KARIN: *How to Become an American*. Peterborough, NH: Cricket Books 2001
HADDIX, MARGARET PETERSON: *Among the Hidden*. New York: Simon & Schuster 2000
HAMILTON VIRGINIA: *Drylongso*. San Diego: Harcourt 1992
HERRICK, STEVEN: *The Simple Gift*. London: Egmont 2004
HERRICK, STEVEN: *by the river*. Crows Nest/ Australia: Allen & Unwin 2004
HESSE, KAREN: *Letters from Rifka*. New York: Henry Holt 1992
HESSE, KAREN: *Witness*. New York: Scholastic 2001
HESSE, KAREN: *Out of the Dust*. Stuttgart: Klett 2002
HESSE, KAREN: *A Light in the Storm*. New York: Scholastic 2003
HIAASEN, CARL: *Hoot*. New York: Yearling 2006
HINTON, S. E.: *The Outsiders*. New York: Viking Press 1967
HOBBS, WILLIAM: *Crossing the Wire*. New York: Harper Collins 2006
HOBBS, WILLIAM: *Far North*. New York: Harper Collins 1996
HOFMANN, E. T. A. & SENDAK, MAURICE: *The Nutcracker*. New York: Random House 1984
HOOKS, WILLIAM: *Pioneer Cat*. New York: Random House 1988
HORNSCHEMEIER, PAUL: *Mother, Come Home*. Seattle, WA: Fantagraphics Books 2009
HOROWITZ, ANTHONY: *Stormbreaker*. London: Puffin Books 2006
HOROWITZ, ANTHONY & JOHNSTON, ANTONY & KANAKO & YUZURU: *Stormbreaker. The Graphic Novel*. (Alex Rider Series). New York: Penguin 2006
IRWIN, HADLEY: *Kim/Kimi*. New York: Puffin 1988
JACOBSEN, SID & COLON, ERNIE: *The 9/11 Report*. New York: Farrar Straus & Giroux 2006
JARAMILLO, ANN: *La Línea*. Stuttgart: Klett 2008
JAMES, BRIAN: *Zombie Blondes*. New York: Feiwel & Friends 2008

Bibliography

Jiminéz, Francisco: *The Circuit*. Albuquerque: University of New Mexico Press 1997

Jiminéz, Francisco: *Breaking Through*. Sandpiper 2002

Johnson, Angela: *The First Part Last*. New York: Simon & Schuster 2003

Kadohata, Cynthia: *Kira-kira*. New York: Alladin Paperbacks 2004

Kästner, Erich: *Emil und die Detektive*. Heidelberg: Dressler 1929

Keeping, Charles: *Through the Window*. New York: F. Watts 1970

Kozar, Richard: *Daniel Boone and the Exploration of the Frontier*. Philadelphia: Chelsea House 2000

Lahiri, Jumpha: *Interpreter of Maladies*. New York: Houghton Mifflin 1999

Larson, Kirby: *Hattie Big Sky*. New York: Delacorte 2007

Lawrence, Jacob: *The Great Migration. An American Story*. New York: Harper Collins 1995

Lawrence, Jacob: *Harriet and the Promised Land*. New York: Aladdin 1997

L'Engle, Madeleine: *A Wrinkle in Time*. New York: Square Fish 2007

Lester, Julius: *A Day of Tears*. New York: Hyperion 2007

Levine, Gail Carson: *Ella Enchanted*. New York: HarperTeen 2004

Levitin, Sonia: *Silver Days*. New York: Aladdin 1992

Levitin, Sonia: *Boom Town*. London: Orchard Books 1998

Levoy, Myron: *Alan and Naomi*. Stuttgart: Klett 1994

Levy, Elizabeth: *Frankenstein Moved In On The Fourth Floor*. New York: Harper Collins 1994

Levy, Elizabeth: *Dracula Is A Pain In The Neck*. New York: Scholastic 1997

London, Jack: *The Call of the Wild*. (Retold by clemen, gina d.b). Genoa: Black Cat 2002

Lorbiecki, Marybeth & Diaz, David: *Just One Flick of a Finger*. New York: Dial Books 1996

Lowry, Lois: *Looking Back. A Book of Memories*. Boston: Houghton Mifflin 1986

Lowry, Lois: *The Giver*. Stuttgart: Klett 1999

Lutzeier, Elizabeth: *Bound for America*. Oxford: Oxford University Press 2002 (new edition)

Macauly, David: *The Way Things Work*. London: Dorling Kindersley, 1988

Magorian, Michelle: *Good Night Uncle Tom*. New Zealand: Topeka Bindery 1999

Mahy, Margaret & Allen, Jonathan: *The Great Man-eating Shark*. London: New ed. Puffin 1995

Manning, Matthew K.: *Marvel Heroes Greatest Battles*. New York: DK 2008

Marzollo, Jean & Sims, Blanche: *Soccer Sam*. New York: Random House,1989

Meyer, Stephenie: *Twilight (Saga)*. London: Little Brown Book Group 2008

Milne, John (Ed.). *Seven Stories of Mystery and Horror*. München: Hueber 2005

Miyazaki, Hayao: *Howl's Moving Castle*. Vol. I. VIZ Media LLC 2005

Moeri, Louise: *Save Queen of Sheba*. New York: Puffin 1994

Mucci, Michael & Haliar, Bill: *Dracula* (Action Classics). NewYork: Sterling 2008

Munoz Ryan, Pam: *Esperanza Rising*. New York: Scholastic 2000

Murphy, Claire Rudolf: *Gold Rush Winter*. New York: Random House 2002

Myers, Walter Dean: *Bad Boy*. New York: Harper Collins 2002

Myers, Walter Dean: *Monster*. Stuttgart: Klett 2003

Myers, Walter Dean: *Sunrise over Fallujah*. New York: Scholastic 2008

Myrick, Leland: *Missouri Boy*. New York: First Second Books 2006

NAIDOO, BEVERLEY: *The Other Side of Truth*. New York: Amistad 2002

NAYLOR, PHYLISS REYNOLD: *Sang Spell*. New York: Aladdin 1998

NEEDLE, JAN & STOKER, BRAM: *Bram Stoker's Dracula*. London: Walker Books 2004

PANZER, NORA (Ed.). *Celebrate America in Poetry and Art*. New York: Hyperion Books for Children 1994

PARKER, LEWIS K.: *Why Mexican Immigrants Came to America*. New York: Rosen 2003

PATERSON, KATHERINE: *Lyddie*. London: Puffin 1992

PATON, JILL WALSH: *Parcel of Patters*. New York: Farrar Straus & Giroux 1986

PAUL, KORKY & TZANNES, ROBERT: *Professor Puffendorf's Secret Potions*. Oxford: Oxford University Press 1992

PAUL, KORKY & TZANNES, ROBERT: *Professor Puffendorf's Secret Potions*. Simplified edition: Oxford: Oxford University Press 1996

PAULSEN, GARY: *Hatchet*. New York: Bradbury Press 1987

PAULSEN, GARY: *Soldier's Heart*. New York: Dell 1998

PAULSEN, GARY: *Lawn Boy*. New York: Random House 2007

PILKEY, DAVE: *Captain Underpants and the Preposterous Plight of the Purple Potty People*. New York: Scholastic 2006

PICOULT, JODI: *Wonder Woman. Love and Murder*. New York: DC Comics 2007

POE, EDGAR ALLAN: *Tales of Mystery and Terror*. New York: Waldman Publ. 2008

POE, EDGAR ALLAN: *The Tell-Tale Heart and Other Writings by Edgar Allan Poe*. New York: Bantam 1984

PRELUTSKY, JACK & LOBEL, ARNOLD: *The Random House Book of Poetry for Children*. New York: Random House, 1983

PULLMAN, PHILIP: *His Dark Materials. Trilogy*. New York: Scholastic 1995–2000

RAI, BALI: *Dream On*. Edinburgh: Barrington Stoke 2004

RAI, BALI: *(Un)arranged Marriage*. Stuttgart: Klett 2007

RAY, DEBORAH KOGAN: *Down the Colorado*. Farrar, Straus & Giroux 2007

RATHMAN, PEGGY: *Officer Buckle and Gloria*. New York: Scholastic 1995

REES, CELIA: *Witch Child*. London: Bloomsbury 2000

REES, CELIA: *Witch Child*. Stuttgart: Klett 2004 (Easy Readers)

ROSEN, MICHAEL & BLAKE, QUENTIN: *Sad*. London: Walker Books 2004

ROCKWOOD, JOYCE: *To Spoil the Sun*. New York: Henry Holt 1994

ROSTKOWSKI, MARGARET I.: *After the Dancing Days*. New York: Harper Collins 1988

ROWLING, J. K.: *Harry Potter and the Philosopher's Stone*. London: Bloomsbury 2000

RYAN, MICHAEL: *Teenage Mutant Ninja Turtles. It's a Shell of a Town*. Los Angeles: Tokyopop 2004

SACHAR, LOUIS: *Holes*. Stuttgart: Klett 2002

SACHAR, LOUIS: *Sideways Stories from Wayside School*. New York: Harper Collins 2003

SALINGER, J. D.: *The Catcher in the Rye*. New York: Bantam Books 1951

SAUNDERS, CATHERINE: *Star Wars. The Story of Darth Vader*. (DK readers level 3). London: DK, 2008

SAUNDERS, CATHERINE: *Spiderman. The Amazing Story*. New York: DK, 2006 (Level 1)

SCIESZKA, JON (Ed.): *Guys Write For Guys Read*. New York: Viking 2005

SELZNICK, BRIAN: *The Invention of Hugo Cabret*. New York: Scholastic 2008

SENDAK, MAURICE: *Pierre*. New York: Harper & Row 1962

SENDAK, MAURICE: *Where the Wild Things Are*. New York: Harper & Row 1984 [1963]

Bibliography

Sendak, Maurice: *In the Night Kitchen.* New York: Harper Collins 1996

Sharmat, Marjorie Weinman & Simont, Marc: *Nate the Great Goes Down in the Dumps.* New York: Dell 1991

Shone, Rob & Spender, Nick: *Rosa Parks. The Life of a Civil Rights Heroine.* New York: Rosen 2006

Smith, Betty: *A Tree Grows in Brooklyn.* New York: HarperCollins 1992 [1943]

Smith, Jeff: *Shazam. The Monster Society of Evil.* New York: DC Comics 2007

Smith, Jeff: *Bone. Out from Boneville.* New York: Scholastic 2005

Smith, Roland: *Zach's Lie.* New York: Hyperion 2001

Smith, Roland: *Zach's Run.* New York: Hyperion 2005

Smith, Roland: *The Last Lobo.* New York: Hyperion 1999

Smith, Roland: *Thunder Cave.* New York: Hyperion 1997

Smith, Roland: *Elephant Run.* New York: Hyperion 2007

Spiegelman, Art & Mouly, Francoise (Eds.): *It was a Dark and Silly Night. Comics by Lemony Snicket, William Joyce, Neil Gaiman and more.* New York: Harper Collins 2003

Spiegelman, Art & Mouly, Francoise (Eds.): *Folklore & Fairy Tale Funnies.* New York: HarperCollins 2000

Spiegelman, Art & Mouly, Francoise (Eds.): *Little Lit.* New York: Puffin Books 2000

Spiegelman, Art: *The Complete Maus.* New York: Random House 1997

Spiegelman, Art: *In the Shadow of No Towers.* New York: Viking 2004

Standerline, Joe: *Stone Cold.* Cheltenham: Nelson Thomas 1999

Stanley, Jerry: *Children of the Dust Bowl.* New York: Crown 1992

Steig, William: *Doctor De Soto.* New York: Farrar, Giroux & Strauss 1982

Steig, William: *Shrek!* New York: Farrar, Giroux & Strauss 1990

Steig, William: *CDB!* New York: Aladdin, 2nd paperback ed. 2005

Steig, William: *CDC?* New York: Farrar, Giroux & Strauss 1984

Stevenson, Robert Louis: *Treasure Island.* München: Langenscheidt 2004

Stine, R. L.: *Goosebumps series 2000.* New York: Scholastic 1999

Stine, R. L.: *Horrorlands Series 2000.* New York: Little Apple 1999

Strasser, Todd: *Can't Get There From Here.* New York: Simon & Schuster 2004

Strasser, Todd (Morton Rhue): *Give a Boy a Gun.* Stuttgart: Reclam 2003

Stratemeyer Syndicate: *Nancy Drew. Starter Set 6.* New York: Grosset & Dunlap 2007

Stratemeyer Syndicate: *The Hardy Boys. Starter Set.* New York: Grosset & Dunlap 2007

Swindells, Robert: *Abomination.* Stuttgart: Klett 2005

Swindells, Robert: *Stone Cold.* Stuttgart: Klett 2009

Tan, Shaun: *The Arrival.* New York: Scholastic 2007

Taylor, Mildred D.: *Roll of Thunder, Hear My Cry.* Penguin: New York 1997

Taylor, Clark & Thomson, Jan Dicks: *The House that Crack Built.* San Francisco: chronicle books 1992

Teitelbaum, Michael: *The Story of the Incredible Hulk.* New York: DK 2003

Thomas, Valerie & Paul, Korky: *Winnie the Witch Collection.* Oxford: Oxford Children's Books 2006

Tolkien, J.R.R & Wenzel, David: *The Hobbit: Graphic Novel.* New York: HarperCollins 1998

Trueman, Terry: *Inside Out.* Alexandria, VA: Tempest 2004

Twain, Mark: *The Adventures of Tom Sawyer.* München: Langenscheidt 2005

UCHIDA, YOSHIKO: *Journey to Topaz*. Berkeley: Heyday Books 2004
UNGERER, TOMI: *The Three Robbers*. New York: Atheneum 1976
VAN ALLSBURG, CHRIS: *The Polar Express*. Boston: Mifflin 1985
VAN DRAANEN, WENDELIN & BIGGS, BRIAN: *Shredderman 1: Secret Identity*. New York: Dell 2006
VAUGHN, BRIAN: *Runaways Saga*. New York: Marvel Comics 2007
WATERS, DANIEL: *Generation Dead*. Hyperion Books 2008
WEATHERFORD, CAROLE BOSTON: *Birmingham, 1963*. Honesdale, PA: Wordsong 2007
WEINSTEIN, LAUREN R.: *Girl Stories*. New York: Henry Holt 2006
WESTALL, ROBERT: *Gulf*. Berlin: Cornelsen 1999
WHEELAN, GLORIA: *Homeless Bird*. New York: Harper Collins 2000
WHITE, ELLEN EMERSON: *Where Have All the Flowers Gone: the Diary of Molly MacKenzie Flaherty*. New York: Simon & Schuster 2002
WIESNER, DAVID: *Tuesday*. Wilmington, MA: Clarion Books 1998
WILDER, LAURA INGALLS: *Little House in the Big Woods*. New York: Harper Collins 1994 [1932]
WINDHAM, RYDER: *Star Wars. Galactic Crisis!* (DK readers level 4). London: DK 2005
WOLFF, VIRGINIA EUWER: *Make Lemonade*. New York: Scholastic 1994
WOLFF, VIRGINIA EUWER: *True Believer*. New York: Atheneum 2001
WRIGHT, RICHARD: *Black Boy*. (Easy reader) Stuttgart: Klett
WOODSON, JACQUELINE: *Locomotion*. New York: Putnam 2003
WYNNE-JONES, DIANA: *Howl's Moving Castle*. New York: HarperCollins 2008
YANG, GENE LUEN: *American Born Chinese*. New York: First Second 2006
YEP, LAURENCE: *Dragonwings*. New York: Harper Collins 1977
YEP, LAURENCE: *The Journal of Wong Ming-Chung*. New York: Scholastic 2000
YOLEN, JANE & COVILLE, BRUCE: *Armageddon Summer*. San Diego: Harcourt 1998
ZOLOTOW, CHARLOTTE & SENDAK, MAURICE: *Mr. Rabbit and the Lovely Present*. Glens Falls/NY: Red Fox Books. New ed. 2002
ZUSAK, MARKUS: *The Book Thief*. New York: Alfred Knopf 2006

Professional films (DVDs)

Batman. The Legend Begins.
  Producers: Anne Luiting, Benjamin Melniker. 110 min. Warner Home Video 2002
Bend it like Beckham.
  Director: Gurinder Chadha. 108 min. Redbus Home Entertainment 2002
Come and See the Paradise.
  Director: Ellen Parker. 38 min. 20th-Century Fox, 1990
Dear America – Letters Home from Vietnam.
  Director: Bill Couturié. 87 min. Hbo Home Video 2005
Dear Nobody.
  Director: Juliet May. 30 min. mini series on BBC 1997
Famous Five.
  ▶ Directors: Peter Duffell, Don Leaver, James Gatward and Mike Connor. 30 min. 26 episode TV series. Southern Television 1978
  ▶ Director: Katrine Hedman. Tyne Tees Television, HTV, Zenith North and ZDF 1996
Good Night Mister Tom
  Director: Jack Gold. 108 min. WGBH Boston Studio. (DVD) 2005
Goosebumps.
  Various Directors. TV series. Hyperion Pictures and Protocol Entertainment in

Bibliography

association with Scholastic Corporation 1995–1998
Harry Potter and the Philosopher's Stone
  Director: Chris Columbus. 145 min. Warner Bros. Pictures 2002
The Golden Compass
  Director: Chris Weitz. 113 min. New Line Home Video 2007
Hoot
  Director: Wil Schreiner. 90 min. New Line Home Video 2006
Goosebumps: One Day at Horrorland
  87 min. 20th Century Fox 2008
Howl's Moving Castle.
  Director: Hayao Miyazaki. 119 min. Walt Disney Home Entertainment 2007
Little House on the Prairie
  Director: Melissa Gilbert. 60 min. Goldhil studio 2003
Man on Wire
  Director: James Marsh. 94 min. Discovery Films 2008
Maria Full of Grace
  Director and writer: Joshua Marston; Producer: Paul Mezey, 101 min. Santa Fe Productions 2004
My Side of the Mountain
  Director: James B. Blark. 100 min. Paramount Pictures 2004
Pete's A Pizza and more William Steig stories (Doctor De Soto, The Amazing Bone).
  Directors: Gary Goldberger, Michael Sporn, Peter Reynolds. 54 min. New Video Group 2004
Paranoid Park
  Director: Gus van Sant. 85 min. High Flyers Films 2008
Roll of Thunder, Hear My Cry
  Director: Jack Smight. 110 min. Tomorrow Entertainment 1978
Rhythm Is It!
  Directors: Thomas Grube, Enrique Sánchez Lansch. 100 min. Boomtownmedia 2004

Shazam!
  Directors: Arnold Laven, Arthur H. Nadel. CBS Television 1974
Shrek
  Directors: Andrew Adamson, Vicky Jenson. 91 min. Universal Pictures 2006
Star Wars Episode VI: Return of the Jedi
  Director: Richard Marquand. 134 min. 20th Century Fox 1983
Stormbreaker
  Director: Geoff Sax. 93 min. Entertainment In: Video 2006
Summer of My German Soldier
  Director: Michael Tuchner. 100 min. NBC 1978
The Boy in the Striped Pyjamas
  Director: Mark Herman. 94 min. Miramax 2008
The Hobbit
  Directors: Jules Bass, Arthur Rankin Jr. 90 min. MGM/Warner Bros. 1977 (2011 film adaptation planned)
The Incredible Hulk
  Director: Louis Leterrier. 112 min. Marvel 2008
The Man Who Walked Between the Towers
  Director: Michael Sporn. 10 min. Scholastic Video Collection 2003
Twilight
  Director: Catherine Hardwicke. 121 min. Summit Entertainment 2008
Wetback
  Director: Arturo Perez Torres. 90 min. Heater Haynes (producer) 2005
Where the Wild Things Are and Other Maurice Sendak Stories
  28 min. Scholastic Video Collection 2001

TV programs
Wordgirl (PBS TV series)
The Magic School Bus

Amateur films of the *Pädagogische Hochschule* Freiburg available from the author
Holes (2005)

The Giver (2006)
Give a Boy a Gun (2007)
(Un)arranged Marriage (2008)

Video and computer games:
Bone: Out from Boneville.
San Rafael: Telltale Games 2005
Bone: The Great Cow Race.
San Rafael: Tellltale Games 2006

Secondary literature

ALTRICHTER, HERBERT & POSCH, PETER: *Lehrerinnen und Lehrer erforschen ihren Unterricht: Unterrichtsentwicklung und Unterrichtsevaluation durch Aktionsforschung.* Köln: Klinkhardt

ANDERSON, NANCY A.: *Elementary Children's Literature. The Basics for Teachers and Parents.* Boston: Pearson, 2nd edition 2006

BACH, GERHARD & TIMM, JOHANNES PETER (Ed.): *Englisch lehren und lernen.* Berlin: Cornelsen 1998

BAUSCH, KARL RICHARD ET AL.: *Handbuch Fremdsprachenunterricht.* Tübingen: A. Francke Verlag, 4th ed. 2003

BENTON, MICHAEL: *Secondary Worlds. Literature Teaching and the Visual Arts.* Maidenhead: Open University Press 1992

BLASINGAME, JIM: "From Wellpinit to Reardan: Sherman Alexie's Journey to the National Book Award". *The ALAN Review* Winter 2008, 69–74

BÖGEL, MIRIAM & HESSE, MECHTHILD: „Der Film Holes. Eine Unterrichtseinheit für die Jahrgangsstufe 10/11." *RAAbits* 42, April 2005a

BÖGEL, MIRIAM & HESSE, MECHTHILD: *Holes. Teacher's Guide.* Stuttgart: Klett, 2005b

BÖGEL, MIRIAM & HESSE, MECHTHILD: *(Un)arranged Marriage. Teacher's Guide.* Stuttgart: Klett 2008

BREDELLA, LOTHAR: "Die Mitwirkung des Lesers beim Verstehen literarischer Texte und die Aufgaben der Literaturdidaktik". In: CANDLIN, CHRISTOPHER & EDELHOFF, CHRISTOPH: *Verstehen und Verständigung.* Bochum: Kamp 1989

BREDELLA, LOTHAR: *Das Verstehenlehren einer paradoxen Epoche in Schule und Hochschule: The American 1920s.* Bochum: Kamp 1985

BREDELLA, LOTHAR & LEGUTKE, MICHAEL: *Confidence.* Bochum: Kamp 1986

BREDELLA, LOTHAR: *Challenges of Literary Texts in the Foreign Language Classroom.* Tübingen: Narr 1996

BREDELLA, LOTHAR & DELANOY, WERNER (Eds.): *Interkultureller Fremdsprachenunterricht.* Tübingen: Gunter Narr 1999

BREDELLA, LOTHAR: „Literary Texts". In: BYRAM 2000, 375–382

BREDELLA, LOTHAR: *Literarisches und interkulturelles Verstehen.* Tübingen: Gunter Narr 2002

BREDELLA, LOTHAR & BURWITZ-MELZER, EVA: *Rezeptionsästhetische Literaturdidaktik mit Beispielen aus dem Fremdsprachenunterricht Englisch.* Tübingen: Gunter Narr 2004

BREEN, MICHAEL: "Learner Contributions to Task Design". In: CANDLIN & MURPHY, 23–46

BROZO, WILLIAM G.: *To Be a Boy, to Be a Reader: Engaging Teen and Preteen Boys in Active Literacy.* Newark: American Reading Association 2002.

BUCKLY CARTER, JAMES: *Building Literacy Connections with Graphic Novels.* Urbana: NCTE 2007

BURWITZ MELZER, EVA: *Allmähliche Annäherungen. Fiktionale Texte im interkulturellen Fremdsprachenunterricht der Sekundarstufe I.* Tübingen: Gunter Narr 2003

BUSHMAN, JOHN H. & PARKS, KAY HAAS: *Using Young Adult Literature in the English Classroom.* Upper Saddle River, NJ: Merrill 2003

Bibliography

Byram, Michael: "Acquiring Intercultural Communicative Competence: Fieldwork and Experiential Learning". In: Bredella & Delanoy, 358–380

Byram, Michael (Ed.): *Routledge Encyclopedia Of Language Teaching and Learning*. London: Routledge 2000

Burdge, Anthony S.: "Graphic Novels". In: Zipes 3, 166–167

Candlin, Christopher & Murphy, David (Eds.): *Language Learning Tasks*. London: Prentice Hall 1987

Chiu, Ching-Hsien: *Learn to Love Reading. Testing the Influence of Young Adult Literature on Literacy Development*. Saarbrücken: VDM Verlag Dr. Müller 2007

Collins, Tom: „Superheroes" in: Zipes 4: 59

Council Of Europe (Ed.): *Modern Languages: Learning, Teaching, Assessment. A Common European Framework of Reference*. Cambridge: Cambridge University Press 2001

Delanoy, Werner: „Fremdsprachenunterricht als dritter Ort". In: Bredella & Delanoy, 121–159

Deutsches Pisa Konsortium (Ed.): *PISA 2000*. Opladen: Leske & Budrich 2001

Dewey, John: *Experience and Education*. London: Scribner 1997 [1938]

Duncan, Diane: *Teaching Children's Literature. Making stories work in the classroom*. London: Routledge 2009

Eccleshare, Julia: "Portrait of the artist as a gorilla." Guardian Unlimited Books, 29 July 2000. Retrieved Nov. 2, 2008 from www.guardian.co.uk/books/2000/jul/29/booksforchildrenandteenagers

Field, Syd: *The Screenwriter's Workbook*. New York: Dell, 1984

Foster, John: "Comic Books". In: Zipes 1, 334–339

Gaschke, Susanne: „Das Phänomen 'Harry Potter': Globalisierung kann angenehm und sehr anspruchsvoll sein". *Die Zeit*, 30, 19.7. 2007

Glatzle, Veronica et al.: *Abomination*. Stuttgart: 47 RAAbits Juli 2006

Goodnow, Cecilia: "Teens buying books at fastest pace in decades." *Seattle Post-Intelligencer*, March 7, 2007

Grilli, Giorgia: "Gaiman, Neil": In: Zipes 2, 113f.

Hallet, Wolfgang & Nünning, Ansgar (Eds.): *Romandidaktik. Theoretische Grundlagen, Methoden, Lektüreanregungen*. Trier: Wissenschaftlicher Verlag 2009

Hahn, Daniel & Flynn, Leonie (Eds.): *The Ultimate Book Guide*. London: A & C Publishers 2004

Harrison, Barbara & Maguire, Gregory (Eds.): *Innocence & Experience. Essays & Conversations on Children's Literature*. New York: Lotthrop, Lee & Shepard Books 1987

Haug, Katja: "'Jungen lieben Erfolgserlebnisse'. Interview mit Christine Garbe über die Leseförderung von Jungen". 22.11.06. Retrieved Mar. 15, 2009 from file:///H:/leseforschung%20garbe.htm

Hayn, Judith & Sherrill, Deborah: "Female Protagonists in Multicultural Young Adult Literature: Sources and Strategies". ALAN Review, vol. 25/1, Fall 1996. Retrieved Mar. 18, 2009 from Http://scholar.lib.vt.edu/ejournals/ALAN/fall96/f96-09-Hayn.html

Hendrickson, Linnea: "Hinton, S.E.". In: Zipes 2, 232–233

Hesse, Mechthild: *The Giver. Teacher's Guide*. Stuttgart: Klett 1999

Hesse, Mechthild & Putjenter, Britta: *Dear Nobody. Teacher's Guide*. Stuttgart: Klett 2000

Hesse, Mechthild: *Jugendliteratur als Schreiblehre*. Tübingen: Gunter Narr 2002a

Hesse, Mechthild: *Out of the Dust. Teacher's Guide*. Stuttgart: Klett 2002b

Hesse, Mechthild: *Seedfolks. Teacher's Guide*. Stuttgart: Klett 2002c

HESSE, MECHTHILD: "Hoffnung in amerikanischen Ghetto: ein multikultureller ‚community garden'". *Der Fremdsprachliche Unterricht Englisch* 36.59/2002d: 14–18

HESSE, MECHTHILD (Ed.): *Juvenile Fiction Book Reviewss*. Friedrichsdorf: Philipp-Reis-Schule 2003

HESSE, MECHTHILD: "Recent Good Children's and Teenage Literature for Today's English Learners." In: *Praxis Fremdsprachenunterricht* 3/ 2007: 66–70

HESSE, MECHTHILD: "Border experience". *Praxis Englisch* 6/2008, 47–48

HESSE, MECHTHILD: "Zeitgenössische Jugendromane im Unterricht". In: *Handbuch Romandidaktik* 2009a

HESSE, MECHTHILD: "Disciplining Boys with Marriage Arrangements" – Bali Rai's *(Un)arranged Marriage* in the EFL Classroom". In: Heidelberg: Winter 2009b

HITCHENS, CHRISTOPHER: "Oxford's Rebel Angel" *Vanity Fair*, Oct. 2002. Retrieved July 2008 from http://www.vanityfair.com/culture/features/2002/10/hitchens 200210

HINTZ, CARRIE & OSTRY, ELAINE (Eds.): *Utopian and Dystopian Writing for Children and Young Adults*. New York: Routledge 2003

HOOG ET AL.: *Superman und Golem. Der Comic als Medium jüdischer Erinnerung*. Frankfurt: Stadt Frankfurt 2008

HUNFELD, HANS: *Englischunterricht: Literatur 5–10*. München: Urban & Schwarzenberg 1982

HUNFELD, HANS: *Fremdheit als Lernimpuls. Skeptische Hermeneutik – Normalität des Fremden – Fremdsprache Literatur*. Klagenfurt: Drava 2004

HUNT, JONATHAN: "Borderlands. Redefining the Young Adult Novel". *The Horn Book Magazine*, March/April 2007. Retrieved Nov. 18, 2008 from www.hbook.com/magazine/articles/2007/mar07_hunt.asp.

HUNT, PETER (Ed.): *Literature for Children*. London: Routledge 1992

HUNT, PETER (Ed.): *Children's Literature. An Illustrated History*. Oxford: Oxford University Press 1995

HUNT, PETER (Ed.): *International Companion of Children's Literature*. London: Routledge 1996

HUNT, PETER (Ed.): *Understanding Children's Literature*. London: Routledge 1999

HUNT, PETER: *Children's Literature*. Oxford: Blackwell 2001

HUNT, PETER (Ed.): *International Companion Encyclopedia of Children's Literature*. Vol. 1 & 2. London: Routledge 2004

ISAAC, MEGAN LYNN: "Short Story". In: ZIPES 3: 453

ISER, WOLFGANG: *Der Akt des Lesens*. München: Wilhelm Fink Verlag 1972

JÄGER, ANJA: *Interkulturelles Lernen mit Literatur und szenischen Verfahren im aufgabenorientierten Englischunterricht*. Pädagogische Hochschule Freiburg 2009 (Dissertation not yet published)

JOOSEN, VANESSA: „Realism". In: ZIPES 3, 328

ISAAC, MEGAN LYNN: "Short Story". In: ZIPES 3: 452–454

KAST, BERND: *Jugendliteratur im kommunikativen Deutschunterricht*. München: Langenscheidt 1985.

KASTEN, WENDY C. ET AL.: *Living Literature. Using Children's Literature to Support Reading and Language Arts*. Upper Saddle River: Pearson 2005

KESSLER, CAROLYN (Ed.): *Cooperative Language Learning. A Teacher's Resource Book*. London: Prentice Hall 1992.

KIEWEG, WERNER: „Schreibprozesse gestalten, Schreibkompetenz entwickeln". *Der fremdsprachliche Unterricht Englisch* 07/2008, 2–8

KIEWEG, WERNER: „Workshop Writing". *Der fremdsprachliche Unterricht Englisch* 07/2008, 38–44

Bibliography

Kist, Heiko: *Leseförderung im Unterricht der Realschule dargestellt am Beispiel von „Professor Puffendorf's Secret Potions" – A Classroom Project.* Unveröffentlichte wissenschaftliche Hausarbeit. Pädagogische Hochschule, Freiburg 2006

Kist, Heiko: *La Linéa. Teacher's Guide.* Stuttgart: Klett 2009

Knowles, Elizabeth & Smith, Martha: *Boys and Literacy. Practical Strategies for Librarians, Teachers and Parents.* Westport: Libraries Unlimited 2005

Kramsch, Claire: *Context and Culture in Language Teaching.* Oxford: Oxford University Press 1993

Krashen, Stephen D.: *Second Language Acquisition and Language Learning.* Oxford: Pergamon Press 1981

Krashen, Stephen D.: *The Power of Reading. Insights from Research.* Portsmouth N.H.: Heinemann, 2nd ed. 2004 [1993]

Kullmann, Thomas: *Englische Kinder- und Jugendliteratur.* Berlin: Schmidt 2008.

Kushner, Tony: *The Art of Maurice Sendak. 1980 to the Present.* New York: Harry N. Abrams 2003

Küppers, Almut & Quetz, Jürgen (Eds.): *Motivation Revisited. Festschrift für Gerd Solmecke.* Berlin: LIT Verlag 2006

Küppers, Almut: "Von Harry Potter lernen heißt: Lesen lernen. Von den Erkenntnissen der Lesesozialisationsforschung und deren Bedeutung für den Fremdsprachenunterricht". *Fremdsprachenunterricht*, 5/2001, 324–31

Marquis, Claudia: " Hinton, S.E." In: Zipes 2: 232

Latrobe et al.: *The Children's Literature Dictionary: Definitions, Resources and Learning Activities.* New York: Neal-Schuman 2002

Legutke, Michael & Thomas, Howard: *Process and Experience in the Language Classroom.* London: Longman 1991

Legutke, Michael: „Projektunterricht". In: Bausch et al., 259–263

Legutke, Michael, Müller-Hartmann, Andreas & Schocker-v. Ditfurth, Marita: *Teaching English in the Primary School.* Stuttgart: Klett 2009

Legutke, Michael & Schmidt, Sebastian: „Nick Hornbys Slam: Szenarien für ein Theaterprojekt". in: Hallet, Wolfgang & Nünnning, Ansgar: 147–164

Lummel, Michael: "Mehr lesen, mehr verstehen – neue Wege der Leseförderung". *Praxis Fremdsprachenunterricht* 6, 2008, 7–12

Marler, Regina: "They Die and Diet." *New York Times Book Review*, July 13, 2008

McCafferty et al (Eds.): *Cooperative Learning and Second Language Teaching.* Cambridge: Cambridge University Press 2006

McKee, Gabriel: "The Gospel According to Science Fiction". Retrieved Mar. 9, 2009 from http:www.city-journal.org

Mertens, Marian & Rombach, Carina: Unpublished project report *(Un)arranged Marriage* PH Freiburg 2009

Millard, Elaine: *Differently Literate: Boys, Girls, and the Schooling of Literacy.* London: Falmer Press 1997

Millard, Elaine: "How Boys' and Girls' Experiences of Reading Shape Their Writing." In: Evans, Janet (Ed.). *Writing in the Elementary Classrooms: A Reconsideration.* Portsmouth: Heinemann 2001

Mukherjee, Joybato: "Unity in Diversity: The Indian Kaleidoscope in the EFL Classroom". 143–151. In: Delanoy, Werner & Volkmann, Laurenz (Eds.): *Cultural Studies in the EFL Classroom.* Heidelberg: Winter 2006

Müller-Hartmann, Andreas: „Auf der Suche nach dem ‚dritten Ort': Das Eigene und das Fremde im virtuellen Austausch über literarische Texte". In: BREDELLA & DELANOY, 160–182

MÜLLER-HARTMANN, ANDREAS & RICHTER, ANNETTE: „Von Holden Caulfield zu Ahn Joo. Multikulturelle Jugendliteratur". In: *Der Fremdsprachliche Unterricht Englisch* 36.59/2002a: 4–11

MÜLLER-HARTMANN, ANDREAS & RICHTER, ANNETTE: „Neue multikulturelle Jugendliteratur." In: *Der Fremdsprachliche Unterricht Englisch* 36.59/2002b: 12–14

MÜLLER-HARTMANN, ANDREAS & SCHOCKER-V. DITFURTH, MARITA: *Introduction to the Teaching of English.* Stuttgart: Klett 2004.

NAHSON, CLAUDIA J.: *The Art of William Steig.* New Haven: Yale University Press 2007

NATIONAL ENDOWMENT FOR THE ARTS: *Reading on the Rise.* 2009 http://www.nea.gov/research/ReadingonRise.pdf retrieved April 26 2009

NATIONAL ENDOWMENT FOR THE ARTS: *Reading at Risk.* 2004 http://www.nea.gov/news/news04/ReadingAtRisk.Html retrieved April 26 2009

NEWKIRK, THOMAS: *Misreading Masculinity. Boys, Literacy, and Popular Culture.* Portsmouth: Heineman 2002

NICHOLS, KRISTEN: "Facts and Fictions: Teen Pregnancy in Young Adult Literature". *ALAN Review Summer 2007* http://findarticles.com/p/articles/mi_qa4063/is_200707/ai_n19433872 retrieved March 26, 2009

NIKOLAJEVA, MARIA: "Picture Books", In: ZIPES 3, 247–251

NIKOLAJEVA, MARIA: "Fantasy". In: ZIPES 2, 58–63

NISSEN, RUDOLF: „Wozu Jugendbücher – und welche? Überlegungen, Leseempfehlungen und Auswahlbibliographie." In: *Der Fremdsprachliche Unterricht* 22.91/1988, 4-9

NISSEN, RUDOLF: *Nissens Almanach. 111 Leseempfehlungen für Schule und Haus.* Hamburg: ELT 1985

NISSEN, RUDOLF: *Nissens Neuer Almanach.* Hamburg: Petersen 1995

NODELMAN, PERRY & REIMER, MAVIS: *The Pleasure of Children's Literature.* Boston: Allyn & Bacon 2003 [1992]

NÜNNING, ANSGAR & SURKAMP, CAROLA: *Englische Literatur unterrichten. Grundlagen und Methoden.* Seelze: Klett Kallmeyer 2006

NÜNNING, ANSGAR & SURKAMP, CAROLA: *Englische Literatur unterrichten/ 2. Unterrichtsmodelle und Materialien.* Seelze: Klett Kallmeyer 2009

NÜNNING, ANSGAR: „Literatur ist, wenn das Lesen wieder Spaß macht!" In: *Der Fremdsprachliche Unterricht Englisch* 31.27/1997, 4–12.

OSBORN, SUNYA: "Picture Books for Young Adult Readers". *The ALAN Review*, Vol. 28, Number 3, 2001. Retrieved Mar.19, 2009 from http://scholar.lib.vt.edu/ejournals/ALAN/v28n3/osborn.html

PARINI, JAY (Ed.): *American Literature.* Vol. 4. Oxford: Oxford University Press 2004

PAUL, LISSA: "Books of Instruction". In ZIPES 1, 185–188

PAWUK, MICHAEL: *Graphic Novels. A Genre Guide to Comic Books, Manga, and More.* Westport: Libraries Unlimited 2007

PETERS, CHRISTOPH & UNTERWEGS, FRIEDRICH-K.: 2005. "Nichts Neues zu vermelden? Eine Umfrage zum Einsatz von Literatur im Englischunterricht der Sekundarstufe II". In: *Neusprachliche Mitteilungen aus Wissenschaft und Praxis* 59, Heft 3: 19–25

PIEPER, IRENE ET AL.: *Lesesozialisation in schriftfernen Lebenswelten: Lektüre und Mediengebrauch von Hauptschüler-Innen.* München: Juventa 2004

PLOTINSKY, BENJAMIN A.: "How Science Fiction Found Religion". Retrieved

Bibliography

Mar. 9, 2009 from http:www.city-journal.org

POTT, SIMONE: 2007. „Mit Schlafsack und Taschenlampe." In: *Der Fremdsprachliche Unterricht Englisch* 41.89: 24–28.

REALSCHULE ENGER: *Lernkompetenz III. Bausteine für kooperatives und kommunikatives Lernen 7.–9. Schuljahr.* Berlin: Cornelsen 2005

REYNOLDS, KIMBERLEY ET AL.: *Frightening Fiction.* London: Continuum 2001

RICH, MOTOKO: "Literacy Debate, R U Really Reading?" *New York Times*, 7/27/08 p. 1, 16–17. Retrieved Aug. 2, 2008 from

RICH, MOTOKO: "Fiction Reading Increases for Adults?" *New York Times*, 1/12/09 Retrieved April 18, 2009 from http://www.nytimes.com/2009/01/12/books/ reading.html

ROCHMAN, HAZEL: "Harriet and the Promised Land". Retrieved Mar. 11, 2009 from amazon.com

ROSENBLATT, LOUISE: "On the Aesthetic as the Baisc Model of the Reading Process". In: GARVIN, H. R. (ed): *Theories of Reading, Looking, and Listening.* Lewisburg: Buckning University Press, 17–31

RÖLLICH-FABER, URSULA: „Mangelware Motivation in der Mittelstufe: Haben Maniac Magee, Stargirl und Harry Potter eine Chance?", 165–174. In: KÜPPERS & QUETZ: (Eds.). *Motivation Revisited. Festschrift für Gerd Solmecke.* Berlin: LIT Verlag 2006

RÖLLICH-FABER, URSULA: *Literatur-Kartei Englisch zu den Jugendbüchern J. K. Rowlings ‚Harry Potter'. Lernstationen zu den Bänden 1–4.* Mühlheim: Verlag an der Ruhr 2003

SAPON-SHEVIN ET AL.: "Cooperative Learning and Inclusion". Retrieved Feb. 17, 2009 from Http://www.co-operation.org/pages/overviewpaper.html.

SAX, LEONARD: *Why Gender Matters.* New York: Broadway Books 2005

SCHICKINGER, JÜRGEN: "Der Aufbruch in die Fremde. Comic, Jugendbuch, Bildroman: Shaun Tans 'Ein neues Land' passt in keine Schublade." *Badische Zeitung* 9.8.08

SENDAK, MAURICE: *Caldecott & Co: Notes on Books & Pictures.* Toronto: The Noonday Press 1988

SENF, CAROLIN ET AL.: "Soccer Sam". Eine Englischlektüre über Sport und dessen Integrationswert." *Praxis Englisch* 3/2008, 12–16

SMITH, MICHAEL W. & WILHELM, JEFFREY D.: *Going with the Flow. How to Engage Boys (and Girls) in Their Literacy Learning.* Portsmouth: Heinemann 2006

SMITH, MICHAEL W. & WILHELM, JEFFREY D.: *Reading Don't Fix no Chevys. Literacy in the Lives of Young Men.* Portsmouth: Heinemann 2002

SPIELER, CLAUDIA: *Bend it Like Beckham. Teacher's Guide.* Stuttgart: Klett 2006

SURKAMP, CAROLA & ROSWITHA HENSELER: „Leselust statt Lesefrust. Lesemotivation in der Fremdsprache Englisch fördern." In: *Der Fremdsprachliche Unterricht Englisch* 2007 41.89: 2–19

TABBERT, REINBERT: „Jugendbücher auf Englisch." *Der fremdsprachliche Unterricht Englisch* 29/1997a, 4–9

TABBERT, REINBERT: „Bildergeschichten von Raymond Briggs." *Der fremdsprachliche Unterricht Englisch* 29/1997b, 19–22

TAHLER, ENGELBERT: *Teaching English Literature.* Paderborn: Schöningh 2008

TEICHMANN VIRGINIA: „Kreatives Schreiben". In: BACH & TIMM (Eds.), 250–257

TODOROV, TZVETAN: *Einführung in die phantastische Literatur.* Frankfurt/M: Ullstein 1975

TOLKIEN, J. R. R.: "On Fairy Stories." In: TOLKIEN: *Tree and Leaf*, 11–70, London: Allen and Unwin 1964

TOTARO, REBECCA CAROL NOEL: "Suffering in Utopia: Testing the Limits in Young Adult Novels". In: HINTZ, CARRIE & OSTRY, ELAINE (Eds.): *Utopian and Dystopian Writing for Children and Young Adults*. New York: Routledge 2003, 127–138

UR, PENNY: *A Course in Language Teaching*. Cambridge: Cambridge University Press 2003 [1996]

VOLKMANN, LAURENZ: "Unterhaltungsliteratur – Schülerinnen und Schüler beim Lesen begleiten". *Der fremdsprachliche Unterricht Englisch* 48/2000, 4–11

VYGOTSKY, LEV: *Mind in Society*. Cambridge: Harvard University Press, 1978

WATSON, VICTOR: *The Cambridge Guide to Children's Books in English*. Cambridge: Cambridge University Press 2001

WILHELM, JEFFREY D.: *Action Strategies for Deepening Comprehension*. New York: Scholastic 2002

WILHELM, JEFFREY D.: *You Gotta Be the Book. Teaching Engaged and Reflective Reading With Adolescents*. 2nd ed., New York: Teacher College Press 2007 [1997]

WILLIAMS, MARION & BURDEN, ROBERT L.: *Psychology for Language Teachers*. Cambridge: Cambridge University Press 1997

ZIPES, JACK (Ed.): *The Oxford Encyclopaedia of Children's Literature*, Vol. 1–4. Oxford: Oxford University Press 2006

Urls

Ghost stories. (2001). In: *The Cambridge Guide to Children's Books in English*. Cambridge: Cambridge University Press. Retrieved Nov. 21, 2008 from http://proxy.stetson.edu:2407/entry/5708621/.

Fantasy. (2005). In: *Continuum Encyclopedia of Children's Literature*. London: Continuum. Retrieved Nov. 21, 2008 from http://proxy.stetson.edu:2407/entry/5659618

Mystery And Detective Stories. (2005). In: *Continuum Encyclopedia of Children's Literature*. London: Continuum. Retrieved Nov. 21, 2008 from http://proxy.stetson.edu:2407/entry/5660045

Realistic Fiction. (2005). In: *Continuum Encyclopedia of Children's Literature*. London: Continuum. Retrieved Nov. 21, 2008 from http://proxy.stetson.edu:2407/entry/5660158

Urls:
Graphic novels
http://www.princetonlibrary.org
http://www.scholastic.com/graphix/Scholastic_BoneDiscussion.pdf

About Anthony Browne
www.guardian.co.uk/books/2000/jul/29/booksforchildrenandteenagers

Excellent source for YA research
www.scils.rutgers.edu/~kvander/

Lois Lowry
http://www.loislowry.com

Wordgirl
pbskidsgo.org/wordgirl

Gender
file:///H:/leseforschung%20garbe.htm

About FELDSTEIN, AL & KRIGSTEIN, BERNARD: Master Race
http://www.bkrigstein.com/comics.html

Index

Abela	38, 47
Abomination	36 50, 94, 127
Action	23, 27, 75
Action comics	25
Action strategies	114, 115
Adventure stories	15, 25, 47ff., 69
African-Americans	22, 38f.
A Gathering of Flowers	68
A Ghost Story	60
Alex Rider	66
Alan and Naomi	43
Alice in Wonderland	61
Alienation	38
A Light in the Storm	43
Always Running	76
Amargeddon Summer	15
America	9, 41, 44, 46, 75, 116
American Born Chinese	32
Among the Hidden	15, 57f.
Anderson, M. T.	18
Animal fantasy	122
Armstrong, Jennifer	23
Art (picture book)	21ff.
Artemis Fowl	55
Asian-Americans	32, 38
A Swift Pure Cry	51
A Tree Grows in Brooklyn	43
A Wrinkle in Time	17
Audubon	23
Auster, Paul	17
Australia	9
Authentic literature	20, 128
Autobiography	26, 74, 76, 116
Bad Boy	76
Batman	64
Bawden, Nina	50
Bend It Like Beckham	40
Berufsschule	111
Beyond the Great Divide	43
Birmingham	76
Blake, Quentin	35
Blume, Judy	35
Blyton, Enid	49, 51f.
Biography	74ff., 120
Bone: Out of Boneville	31
Book box (see also class library)	117f., 120, 125
Bound for America	43
Boy	76
Boys' stories	69
Boys' reading	9, 13, 16, 122
Breaking Through	38
Briggs, Raymond	26
Brooklyn Follies	17
Browne, Anthony	19, 22, 24, 27, 29, 59
Bruchac, John	44
Bukowski, Charles	116
Bull Run	15, 43, 47
Bunting, Eve	44
Busch, Wilhelm	25
by the river	72
Caldecott Award	28
Call of the Wild	48
Captain Marvel	62, 65
Captain Underpants	116
Carnegie Medal	51
Cartoons	23, 25, 29, 65
Chambers, Aidan	18
Change of perspective	104ff.
Characters	8, 13ff., 18, 24, 34, 37, 43, 52f., 55, 60, 79, 80, 82f., 89, 92
Class library (see also book box)	118
Classics	14, 19, 90, 128
CDB!	29
CDC?	29
"Chick lit."	18, 117
Children of the River	38
Censorship	116
Code Talker	38, 43
Coeducation	15
Coleville, Bruce	56
Comics	6, 14, 21ff., 25ff., 63ff.
Common European Framework of Reference	78
Communication	6, 21, 86, 91
Competences (see skills)	12, 78, 87, 11, 114
Cooper, Susan	58
Cooperative learning	93, 109
Coraline	61
Course books (see textbooks)	8

146

Index

Creative writing	73, 86, 96f.
Creech, Sharon	70, 126
Criteria	10, 12, 77, 118
Cross, Gillian	48
Crossing the Wire	39, 43, 79
Crossover novels	18
Culhane, Kate	60
Dahl, Roald	55, 77
Dali, Salvador	25
Dandelions	44
Day of Tears	43
Dear America	42
Dear Nobody (novel)	15, 36
Defoe, Daniel	48
Der Zauberlehrling	29
Design (picture books)	21ff., 31, 35
Detective fiction	49
Dhami, Narinder	40
Diakité	25
Dialogue	25
Diamond Willow	15, 49f., 69
Diaz, David	37
Dicamillo, Kate	35
Die drei ???	118
Division of labor	92
Doctor De Soto (picture book)	29
Doctor De Soto (film)	31
Doherty, Berlie	36
Dowd, Siobhan	51
Dracula	62
Dracula is a Pain in the Neck	60
Dragonwings	38
Drama	73
Dramatic tension	108
Dramatizing	73, 82, 90, 105, 111, 113
Dream On	41
Duncan, Lois	27, 68
Eisner, Will	26, 31
Ella Enchanted	55
Email exchange	80
Emil und die Detektive	49
Empathy	104ff.
Enactment strategies (see action strategies)	115
Ender's Game	55, 59
Ending	82, 85f., 88, 98, 103
Esperanza	43
Ethnic literature	38, 40, 58, 76
Experience	5, 7, 10, 17, 21, 38, 41, 54, 78, 120
Expert Puzzle	16
Exposition	98, 104
Extensive reading	6, 72, 87f., 89, 114, 129
Fahrenheit 451	68
Fairy tale	98
Famous Five	51
Fantasy	27, 52f.
Far North	48
Fat Little Lit	31, 34
Feed	18
Feedback	112
Feelings	114f.
Feldstein, Al	26
Fiction	10f., 17, 41, 47
French, Fiona	59
First-person narrator	92
Flashback	115
Fleischman, Paul	40, 74
Fleischman, Sid	56
Folklore and Fairy Tale Funnies	31
Forever	35
Forest	23
Frankenstein Moved in on Fourth Floor	60
Frost, Helen	15, 49f., 69
Fundraising	119
Fünf Freunde	118
Gaiman, Neil	61
Galactic	64f.
Gelletly, LeeAnne	75
Gender	13ff.
Generation Dead	54
Genre	7f., 11, 15, 17f., 21, 25ff., 38, 40, 42, 49f., 52f., 55, 63, 67, 69, 73, 75, 79, 82
George, Jean Craighead	48f.
Germans in America	44ff.
Gerstein, Mordicai	75

Index

Ghost stories	60
Giff, Patricia Reilly	32
Girl Stories	33
Girls' stories	69
Girls' reading	6, 14, 16
Give a Boy a Gun	37
Going Solo	76
Gold Rush Winter	43
Graded Readers	
(see also Easy Readers)	64, 128
Graphic novels	21, 26
Greene, Betty	45
Grimm brothers	59
Gulf	43
Guys Write for Guys Read	69
Gymnasium	8, 104, 111, 114
Haddix, Margret Peterson	15, 57
Hague, Michael	60
Haliar, Bill	62
Ham on Wire	116
Harriet and the Promised Land	39
Harry Potter	8, 18, 53, 60
Hatchet	48
Hattie Big Sky	43
Hauptschule	8f., 75
Heneghan, James	96, 126
Herrick, Steven	72
Hesse, Karen	32, 43, 69, 71
Hiaason, Carl	48
Hinton. S. E.	35
His Dark Materials	18f., 53, 55
Historical fiction	41ff.
History of teaching literature	7, 19, 87
Hitchcock, Alfred	50
Hobbs, William	39
Holes	50, 97ff., 100, 103, 114
Homeless Bird	40
Hooks, William K.	44
Horrible History	75
Horror stories	52, 60
Horror	13, 26, 60ff.
Hoot (novel)	48
Hoot (film)	48
Hornschemeier, Paul	26
Horowitz, Anthony	49, 66, 69

House of Tailors	33, 43
Howl's Moving Castle	65
How to Become an American	43
Huckleberry Finn	14, 48
Humanistic psychology	86
Humor	90, 114, 117
Humorous story	99
Identification	12, 19, 104ff.
Illegal immigrants	38
Immigration	23f., 26, 38, 43
Implied author	24
Indian-English migrants	38, 43
Individual reading	
(see also silent reading)	15, 117ff., 128
Information books	7, 13f., 68, 75f., 121
Inside Out	36
Intensive reading	72, 84, 88
Intercultural communicative	
competence (ICC)	78
Interior monologue	99
Interpreter of Maladies	81
In the Night Kitchen	28
In the Shadow of no Towers	26
Intercultural communicative	
competence	78f.
Iron Man	63
It Was a Dark and Silly Night	31
Jacobsen	26
Jamarillo, Ann	39
James and the Giant Peach	55
Jane Grey	65
Jazz	59, 93
Jewish-Americans	27, 63
Johnson, Angela	37
Journey to Topaz	43, 46
Julie of the Wolves	49
Just One Flick of a Finger	37
Kafka	17f.
Kästner, Erich	49
Keeping, Charles	23
Keesha's House	15
Kim/Kimi	38
King of Shadows	58

Index

King Kong	59
Kira-Kira	38
Krigstein, Bernard	26
Lahiri, Jumpha	80
La Línea	39, 43, 79f.
Language development	78ff.
Latinos	39, 79
Lawrence, Jacob	39
L'Engle, Madeleine	17
Letters from Rifka	32, 43, 45
Levithin, Sonia	45
Levy, Elizabeth	60
Light reading	116
Listening	90
Little House in the Big Woods	43
Locomotion	70
London Eye Mystery	51
London, Jack	48
Looking Back	76
Lorbiecki, Marybeth	37
Lord of the Flies	114
Love That Dog	70
Lowry, Lois	18, 57, 68, 76, 86
Lyddie	43
McKean, Dave	61
Magorian, Michelle	44
Magnuson, Diana	44
Magritte, René	19, 25
Mahy, Margaret	31
Man on Wire	75
Marzollo, Jean	39
Master Race	26
Maus	26
Max und Moritz	25
Meier, Stephenie	14
Mexican-Americans	41
Migrants	38, 42, 71
Mister Rabbit and the Lovely Present	24
Missouri Boy	32
Miyazaki, Hayao	65
Mother, Come Home	26
Monster	37f.
Morton Rhue (see Strasser, Todd)	37
Moulton, William Marston	63
Mouly, Francoise	31
Mucci, Michael	62
multi-perspective	37, 89
Multicultural novel	38ff., 79
My Dad	27
Myers, Walter Dean	37
My Mum	27
Myrick, Leland	32
My Side of the Mountain	49
Mystery	49f.
Mythology	23
Nancy Drew	50
Nate the Great Goes Down in the Dumps	50
Narration	99
Narrative perspective	15, 39
Narrator	17, 20, 91, 93
Native Americans	38, 76
Nazi Germany	45, 116
Necessary Noise	67f.
Negotiating meaning	85
Newbery Medal	22, 46, 56, 74, 98
New York	26, 29, 45, 59, 63f.
Non-fiction (see also information books)	73
Oates, Joyce Carol	68
Officer Buckle and Gloria	23
Open ending	86
Oklahoma Dust Bowl	71
Oral storytelling	21
Ormerod, Jan	69
Out of the Dust	43, 71
Pädagogische Hochschule Freiburg	109, 120
Parcel of Patterns	41
Parker, Lewis K.	75
Paulsen, Gary	46, 48
Perspective	8f., 19f., 37, 82, 104
Pete's A Pizza	30
Picoult, Jodi	63
Pierre	43
Pioneer Cat	44

Index

PISA study	118
Place	34, 53
Paul, Korky	29
Plot	14, 22, 52, 82, 92, 104
Poe, Edgar Allan	60, 66
Poetry	72, 81
Point of view	11, 23, 43, 95, 103
Problem novel	34
Productive skills	87
Professor Puffendorf's Secret Potion	29
Project	7ff., 42, 104
Pulitzer Prize	26
Pullman, Philip	18f., 53
Rai, Bali	41
Rathman, Peggy	23
Raynolds, Phillis Naylor	58
Reader response theory	19f., 80f., 102
Reading	87
Reading comprehension	87
Reading journal	102f.
Reading motivation	127, 129
Reading strategies	88
Reading-writing-speaking connection	123
Realism	24, 34
Realschule	61, 114, 127
Reception	80
Receptive skills	87
Reluctant readers	71, 116
Rhythm is it	5
Robinson, Charles	44
Robinson Crusoe	48
Rodriguez, Luiz	76
Role play	83, 94, 104, 115, 119
Romance	14, 21, 117
Rosa Parks	76
Rosen, Michael	35
Rowling, J. P.	18, 53
Runaways	52
Ryan, Michael	64
Sachar, Louis	55, 97
Sad	35
Salinger	35
Sang Spell	58
Saunders, Catherine	64
Save Queen of Sheiba	43
Scieszka, Jan	69
School stories	35
Secret Seven	51
Seedfolks	40
Sendak, Maurice	21, 28
Setting	22, 49
Seven Stories of Mystery and Horror	67
Sex and Love	68
Shakespeare, William	60
Shazam	65
Shone, Rob	76
Short stories	67
Shredderman	50
Shrek! (picture book)	31
Shrek! (film)	31
Sideways Stories from Wayside School	55
Silent reading (see also individual reading)	9, 15, 125
Silver Days	45
Simplified readers	20, 128
Simont, Marc	50
Sims, Blanche	39
Sis, Peter	56
Sitting Bull	76
Skellig	56
Skills	7, 73, 87ff., 96
Smith, Jeff	65
Smith, Roland	51
Snow White in New York	59
Soccer Sam	39
Soft Rain	43
Soldier's Heart	43, 46
Space Brat	56
Speaking	91
Speech	73, 93, 95, 102
Spender, Nick	76
Spiderman	64
Spiderwoman	64
Spiegelman, Art	26, 31
Spy story	59, 66
Standerline, Joe	51
Star Wars	64
Steig, William	29, 31
Stevenson, Robert Louis	48

Index

Stone Cold (novel)	51
Stone Cold (play)	51
Stormbreaker	49, 66
Story	7, 13ff., 17ff.
Storytelling	21
Strasser, Todd	37
Style (picture book)	21, 23f.
Summer of My German Soldier	43, 45
Sunrise over Fallujah	43
Super hero	62
Superman	63
Supernatural	52ff., 60
Survival stories	48
Suspense	15, 55
Sweet Valley High	117
Sweet Valley Kids	117
Sweet Valley Twins	117
Swindells, Robert	51
Systematic writing	97, 99
Taboo in YA literature	35
Tan, Shaun	23, 32
Task-based language learning and teaching	81, 83, 86
Tasks	81
Taylor, Clark	33
Teachers	85
Teenage Mutant Ninja Turtles (comic book)	64
Teenage Mutant Ninja Turtles (film)	64
Textbooks	8, 12, 20, 67, 78
The 9/11 Report	26
The Absolutely True Diary of a Part-time Indian	126
The Amazing Bone	30
The Arrival	23, 32
The Babysitter Club	117
The Birchbank House	43
The Book Thief	10, 18
The Boy in the Striped Pyjamas	18
The Braid	69
The Captain's Dog: My Journey With the Lewis and Clark Tribe	43
The Catcher in the Rye	34
The Chronicles of Prydain	55
The Circuit	43
The Code Talker	38, 43
The Contract with God	26
The Dancing Days	43
The Diary of Molly MacKanzie Flaherty	43
The Dragon of Doom	56
The Fantastic Four	64
The First Part Last	37
The Fly and Other Horror Stories	67
The Giver	18, 57, 86
The Great Depression	43, 92
The Great Elephant Chase	48
The Great Man Eating Shark	30
The Great Migration	39
The Hardy Boys	50
The Hatseller and the Monkeys	22, 24
The Hobbit	55
The House that Crack Built	33
The Incredible Hulk	65
The Indian in the Cupboard	55
The Invention of Hugo Cabret	32
The Journal of Wong Ming-Chung	43
The Last Lobo	47f.
The Lion, the Witch, and the Wardrobe	61
The Magic School Bus	74f.
The Man Who Walked Between the Towers (picture book)	75
The Man Who Walked Between the Towers (film)	75
Then Again, Maybe I Won't	35
The New Yorker	29
The Nutcracker	55
The Other Side of Truth	47f.
The Outsiders	35
The Polar Express	23
The Sandman	61
The Simple Gift	15, 71
The Spirit	63
The Three Investigators	50
The Three Robbers	30
The Thuggery Afffair	50
The Tiger Rising	35
The Trail of Tears	43
The True Diary of a Part-Time Indian	38

Index

The 12th Day of July	109
The Watsons Go to Birmingham	43
The Whipping Boy	56
The Winter People	43
The Witch at Blackbird Pond	43
The Witch's Daughter	50
The Uncommon Reader	11
Third place	81
This is All	18
This is the House that Jack Built	33
Thomas, Valerie	29
Thomson Dicks, Jan	33
Through the Window	23
Thunder Cave	47f.
Tolkien, J. R. R.	53, 55
Tomorrowland	67f.
Tom Sawyer	48
To Spoil the Sun	43
Torn Away	97, 105
Townsend Warbler	74
Toy fantasy	55
Trapped	68
True Believer	72
Trueman, Terry	36
Twain, Marc	48
Twilight	8, 14, 54, 60
Tzannes, Robin	29
Uchida, Yoshiko	46
Ultimate Sports	69
(Un)arranged Mariage	113
Ungerer, Tomi	30
USA (see also America)	12, 18, 25, 43ff., 48, 54, 57, 67, 76, 80, 103, 126, 129
Vampire stories	60, 67
Van Allsburg, Chris	23
Van Draanen, Wendelin	50
Vaughan, Brian	52
Verse novels	69f.
Waldorf schools	20
Walsh, Jill Paton	41, 43
Watership Down	55
Weatherford, Carole Boston	76
Weinman, Marjorie Sharmat	50
Weinstein, Lauren R.	33
Whelan, Gloria	40
Where Have all the Flowers Gone	43
Where the Wild Things Are (picture book)	21, 23, 28
Where the Wild Things Are (film)	28
Why Mexican Immigrants Came to America	75
Willy the Dreamer	24
Winnie the Witch	29
Witch Child	43
Witness	43
Wolff, Virginia Euwer	72
Woodson, Jacqueline	68f., 70
Wolverine	64
Wonder Woman	63
Writing (see also systematic writing)	96
Wynne-Jones, Diana	65
Yang, Gene Luen	32
Zindel, Paul	35
Zipes, Jack	9
Zolotow, Charlotte	24
Zombie Blondes	54
Zombie stories	67
Zusak, Markus	19